Serving the Federal Evaluation Market

Strategic Alternatives for Managers and Evaluators

Richard E. Schmidt
Pamela Horst
John W. Scanlon
Joseph S. Wholey

962-24

January 1977

THE URBAN INSTITUTE
WASHINGTON, D.C.

The research and studies forming the basis for this report were conducted pursuant to Contract Number N01-MH-2-0022 (OP), from the U. S. Department of Health, Education and Welfare, Alcohol, Drug Abuse and Mental Health Administration.

The interpretations or conclusions are those of the authors and should not be attributed to the Alcohol, Drug Abuse and Mental Health Administration, the Urban Institute, its trustees, or to other organizations that support its research.

ISBN 87766-184-7

UI 962-24

PLEASE REFER TO URI 17400 WHEN ORDERING

Available from:

Publications Office
The Urban Institute
2100 M Street, N. W.
Washington, D. C. 20037

List price: $4.50

A/76/500

ACKNOWLEDGEMENTS

This report was prepared under a contract with the U. S. Department of Health, Education and Welfare, the Alcohol, Drug Abuse and Mental Health Administration. It is based on work carried out between 1971 and 1975 with the Alcohol, Drug Abuse and Mental Health Administration and its predecessor, the National Institute of Mental Health.

The study team wishes to acknowledge the contribution of Dr. Scott Nelson and Mr. Thomas Kelly of the Alcohol, Drug Abuse and Mental Health Administration. Dr. Nelson, as the head of the Office of Program Planning and Evaluation, guided the study team throughout the final year of this project and added substantially to our insights and many of the ideas contained within this report and prior analyses completed during the year. Mr. Kelly worked with our team closely throughout most of the three years during which we worked with ADAMHA and the National Institute of Mental Health; his contributions have been significant. This project required the study team to work with many different offices and individuals, ADAMHA itself, the National Institute of Mental Health, the National Institute of Drug Abuse, the National Institute of Alcohol Abuse and Alcoholism, the Office of the Assistant Secretary for Health, the Office of the Assistant Secretary for Planning and Evaluation, the Office of the Assistant Secretary for Administration and Management, and the Office of the Assistant Secretary, Comptroller. We wish to acknowledge the cooperation extended to our team by these offices.

Within The Urban Institute, we wish to acknowledge the role played by the project review committee: Ms. Lucile Graham, Mr. Joe Nay, Ms. Leona Vogt and Dr. Donald Weidman. The committee guided the study team through critical reviews of this project.

Ms. Faye Farnsworth, as the project secretary, performed more than ably throughout the project. She handled the major typing load of all of our project reports, including this final report, as well as the many drafts required at each stage of the project. She was assisted on a number of occasions by Jill Bury, Myriam Gaviria, Gwen Mobley and Montina Pyndell.

TABLE OF CONTENTS

	Page
ABSTRACT	
ACKNOWLEDGMENTS	
I. INTRODUCTION	1
A. Purpose of the Report	1
B. Background of the Report	2
C. Organization of the Report	4
II. EVALUATION--PROBLEMS AND FAILURES	5
A. Statement of Problems	5
1. Symptoms of a Problem	5
2. What is the Problem?	6
B. Prior Solutions Have Not Worked	8
1. Examples of Prior Solutions	8
2. Why Prior Solutions Have Not Worked	11
III. A DIFFERENT APPROACH	13
A. Commodities and Needs	13
B. Why Does the Suggested Approach Promise to Resolve the Problems Where Others Have Failed?	17
1. Success Criteria for Evaluation Offices Suggested	17
2. No Arbitrary Models of the Decision-making Process Are Defined	18
3. Market Demand Studies Are Suggested	18
4. Recommendations Are Made to Develop a Federal Evaluation Policy	19
IV. THE THREE FEDERAL MARKETS FOR EVALUATION INFORMATION	21
A. Introduction	21
B. The Individual Consumer Market	22
1. What Is the Mission of Individual Consumers?	22
2. Who Are the Consumers?	23
3. Objectives and Success Criteria for the Evaluation Office Serving the Individual Consumer Market	24
C. The Program Management Market	26
1. What is a Program?	26
2. Who is the Customer?	28
3. Objectives and Success Criteria for the Evaluation Office Serving the Program Management Market	29
D. The Policy Market	30
1. What is a Policy Issue?	30
2. Who is the Customer?	32
3. Objectives and Success Criteria for the Evaluation Office Serving the Policy Market	32
E. Comparison of the Objectives and Success Criteria for the Three Markets	34

Table of Contents (continued) | *Page*

V. SERVING A MARKET FOR FEDERAL EVALUATION | 39
    A. Introduction | 39
    B. The Individual Consumer Market | 39
        1. Defining the Information Needed by the Market | 39
        2. Serving the Market: The Level and Type of Demand Expected | 42
        3. Implications for Organizing an Evaluation Office | 43
    C. The Program Management Market | 46
        1. Defining the Information Needed by the Market | 46
        2. Serving the Market: The Level and Type of Demand Expected | 48
        3. Implications for Organizing an Evaluation Office | 49
    D. The Policy Market | 50
        1. Defining the Information Needed by the Market | 50
        2. Serving the Market: The Level and Type of Demand Expected | 53
        3. Implications for Organizing an Evaluation Office | 54
    E. Comparison of the Requirements Imposed by the Markets | 55

VI. APPLICATION OF THE MARKET APPROACH | 59
    A. Introduction | 59
    B. Using the Market Approach to Guide Evaluation Office Planning | 60
    C. Using the Market Approach to Clarify Debates Between the Evaluation Office and Review Groups | 62
    D. Using the Market Approach to Establish a Federal Evaluation Policy | 64

APPENDIX A
    Assessment of Evaluability | 69

APPENDIX B
    Rapid Feedback Evaluation | 81

APPENDIX C
    Definition of Federal Evaluation Adopted by a DHEW Task Force on Health Evaluation | 91

LIST OF TABLES

Table		Page
1	Objectives and Success Criteria for an Evaluation Office	35
2	Levels of Evidence for Different Uses on Evaluation Office Performance	36
3	Primary Responsibility for Evaluation Office Activities in an Administrative Model	45
4	Estimated Staff Requirements for the Core Evaluation Office Activities	56
5	Preferred Organizational Models for Serving Federal Evaluation Markets	57
6	Additional Staff Requirements for the Organizational Models	57

LIST OF FIGURES

Figure		Page
1	Key DHEW Organizations Referred to in this Report	3

I. INTRODUCTION

A. PURPOSE OF THE REPORT

The purpose of this report is to articulate criteria which can be used to plan, manage, and evaluate government evaluation offices. It will provide evaluators and those who guide, review, or critique their efforts, with a common basis for discussion and debate. It will illustrate that different success criteria frequently imply different resource and organizational requirements for evaluation offices.

The need for such criteria is pointed up by the persistent lack of agreement on what is expected from the growing federal investment in evaluation.[1] Individual evaluation offices often lack even internal agreement on how to measure their own success in terms useful to evaluation office management. Even when agreement is present, they may still lack the methods for such measurement. Moreover, apart from an office's own management needs, some method is needed by which external reviewers can judge evaluation offices in terms which everyone mutually understands and on which, hopefully, they all agree.

In the following pages we provide a beginning point for the resolution of this problem--an approach for organizing evaluation offices and measuring their success in terms of the many individuals and groups they serve. While we recognize the limitations of business analogies in the context of government operations, we have adopted some business terminology as an aid in organizing our argument and have made particular use of the concept of markets for a product. The analogy has strength in the context of federal evaluation because we are talking about measuring the demand for evaluation information and about managing evaluation offices so as to satisfy real demands. We define three markets for evaluation information and discuss the implications of these markets for organizing evaluation offices, measuring their success, and debating the nature and content of a federal evaluation policy.

[1] Roughly $130 million in fiscal 1974. See Genevieve J. Knezo. *Program Evaluation: Emerging Issues of Possible Legislative Concern Relating to Conduct and Use of Evaluation in the Congress and the Executive Branch*, Congressional Research Service, Library of Congress, JK 421, 75-35 SP, November 16, 1974.

B. BACKGROUND OF THE REPORT

The report is based on over four years of work with various evaluation and management organizations within the Department of Health, Education and Welfare.[2] Many of the examples and illustrations used in this report are taken from that experience.[3]

Figure 1 identifies key DHEW organizational units referred to in this report. Each of the three institutes--National Institute on Alcohol Abuse and Alcoholism (NIAAA), National Institute on Drug Abuse (NIDA), and National Institute of Mental Health (NIMH)--administered programs and had their own evaluation offices. Above the institutes were three levels of guidance and review on evaluation: (1) the Alcohol, Drug Abuse and Mental Health Administration's Office for Program Planning and Evaluation (ADAMHA/OPPE), (2) the Assistant Secretary for Health (ASH), and (3) the Assistant Secretary for Planning and Evaluation (ASPE).

---

2. This work is reported in the following documents:
   (a) *Evaluation Planning at the National Institute of Mental Health: A Case History* by Pamela Horst, John W. Scanlon, Richard E. Schmidt and Joseph S. Wholey, Paper 962-13, Washington, D. C., The Urban Institute, 1974.
   (b) "The Forward Plan, Problems and Possibilities for an Effective Alcohol, Drug Abuse and Mental Health Administration Role" by Pamela Horst, John W. Scanlon and Richard E. Schmidt, Washington, D. C., The Urban Institute, November 23, 1974.
   (c) "The Operational Planning System" by Pamela Horst, John W. Scanlon and Richard E. Schmidt, Washington, D. C., The Urban Institute, March 13, 1975.
   (d) "Observations on the Department of Health, Education and Welfare Budget Process" by Pamela Horst, John W. Scanlon and Richard E. Schmidt, Washington, D. C., The Urban Institute, March 27, 1975.
3. The Urban Institute contracted originally with the National Institute of Mental Health in January 1971. In July 1974 ADAMHA replaced NIMH and our work continued with the Alcohol, Drug Abuse and Mental Health Administration's Office of Program Planning and Evaluation.

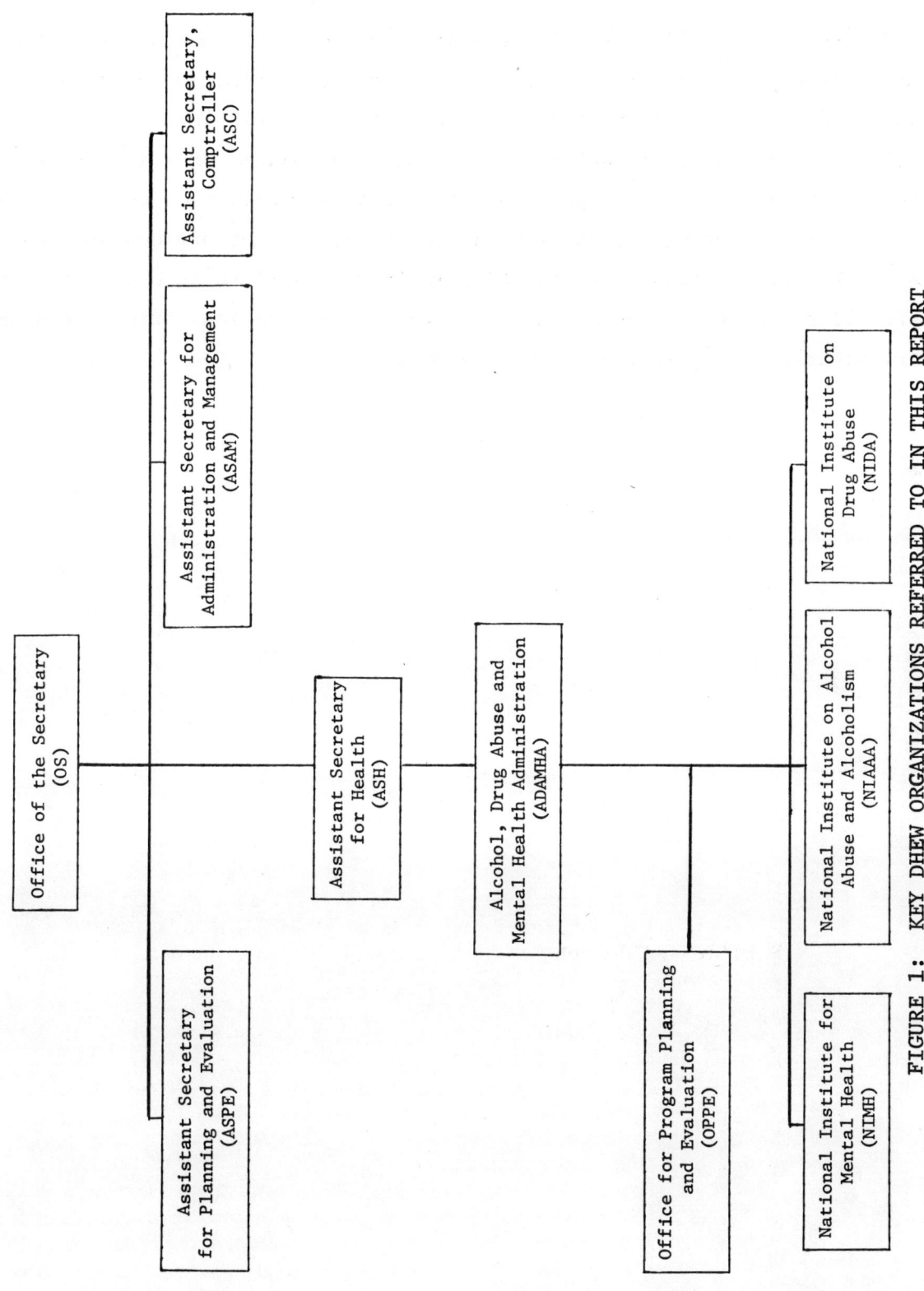

FIGURE 1: KEY DHEW ORGANIZATIONS REFERRED TO IN THIS REPORT

C. ORGANIZATION OF THE REPORT

In Chapter II, which provides the starting point for our subsequent discussion, we explore certain problems facing federal evaluation offices and summarize a number of prior attempts to resolve these problems in whole or in part. In Chapter III, we outline our beginning argument for a different approach. Chapters IV and V provide the central exposition of our approach, defining alternative courses of action open to evaluation offices and tracing some of the organizational and staffing implications of these alternatives. Chapter VI shows how our approach can be used by evaluation offices, evaluation policy makers, and those who review evaluation.

II. EVALUATION--PROBLEMS AND FAILURES

In this chapter we discuss evidence we have observed that problems exist in federal evaluation, what we believe the problems to be, and why prior solutions seem to have failed. We conclude by presenting the beginning argument for a different approach, one which we believe will lead to a solution.

A. STATEMENT OF PROBLEMS

1. SYMPTOMS OF A PROBLEM

Our work with ADAMHA and NIMH encompassed approximately three years. During that time, we observed ADAMHA's evaluation office and the evaluation office of NIMH grapple with two issues: a steady stream of criticism (directed generally at evaluation, although occasionally at NIMH evaluation itself), and uncertainty as to how to organize, plan, and manage its evaluation activities.

The criticism comes in different forms and from different sources. Perhaps the most widespread criticism relates to the utility of evaluation studies to managers and policy makers. Thus, OMB states, "This position paper is written out of a concern that evaluation is not being fully utilized. One of the reasons commonly offered for the underutilization of evaluation studies is the failure of evaluators to provide timely, relevant and accurate information for decision making."[1] In 1973, the office of the Assistant Secretary for Planning and Evaluation (ASPE) noted in its evaluation guidance, "The goal of evaluation is policy and program change. To date, evaluation has only imperfectly achieved that goal."[2] In the past, both the General Accounting Office (GAO) and Congress have also criticized evaluation for its underutilization. Other critics, including academic and nonacademic researchers, have critized evaluation for poor quality. Evaluation offices view much of the criticism as unjustified. They believe that the criticism is often based on arbitrary and ambiguous criteria and on totally different perceptions of (1) the real objectives of evaluation offices, and (2) the limitations (inadequate staffing

---
1. *Evaluation Management:* OMB Position Paper, January 1975.
2. *FY 1973 Health Evaluation Plan:* DHEW/ASPE.

levels, unclear program objectives, constant change) under which such offices operate.

A second major symptom that we have observed is uncertainty and conflict on the part of evaluation offices regarding how to plan and organize their work. The uncertainty and conflict can be seen at every level of DHEW.

- Guidances from DHEW's ASPE telling agencies how to plan and often *what* to plan, are changed annually.

- Individual agency evaluation offices in DHEW and other federal agencies frequently seek contractor assistance in defining evaluation planning approaches—involving, implicitly, the definition of office objectives and, explicitly, ways to achieve those objectives.

- OMB and GAO are now actively involved in developing evaluation planning approaches which imply or explicitly state objectives for evaluation offices different from those some offices have adopted.

- Within DHEW, a health evaluation task force has spent the better part of one year directly or indirectly debating the question of what it is that evaluation offices should be doing.

- In FY 1974, an attempt was made by the NIMH Evaluation Branch to focus its evaluation funds on one subject[3]—evaluation of NIMH's national programs—under conditions which ran counter to the objectives of evaluation held by agency decision makers. The policy was never implemented since it would have restricted the type of studies funded.

Our discussions with evaluation staff at each level, including OMB, suggest, however, that evaluation offices (a) wish to use their resources productively to improve government decision making and operations and (b) are frustrated by too many conflicting demands with no obvious way to choose between them.

2. *WHAT IS THE PROBLEM?*

The problem appears to have two dimensions: (a) evaluation offices have been unable to demonstrate to the outside world that they are successful; and (b) there is no common agreement on what would constitute success, i.e., there is no *operational* federal evaluation policy. Thus both the criticism and the uncertainty in planning are frequently caused by disagreement over objectives and different perceptions of what constitutes adequate evidence of performance on any one objective. Consequently, the debate goes on with different people arguing about different things.

---

3. Pamela Horst, John W. Scanlon, Richard E. Schmidt, and Joseph S. Wholey. *Evaluation Planning at the National Institute of Mental Health: A Case History*, Paper 962-13, Washington, D.C., The Urban Institute, 1974.

a. EVALUATION OFFICE SUCCESS MEASURES

At any given point in time, evaluation offices operate implicitly or explicitly with a given objective in mind, but they are rarely able to claim success for their objective, except by recourse to their own opinion. However, the issue is not whether an individual evaluation office feels that it has achieved success, but whether it can clearly demonstrate to reviewers (ASPE, ASH, OMB, GAO, Congress) that it is successful. A major *problem, then, is the absence of agreed-upon, clearly articulated measures and clearly ordered evidence.* We base this assertion on our observations of evaluation offices in DHEW and other departments over the past five years. We have read the policy guidances and the evaluation plans, participated in evaluation office discussions and planning processes, and worked with DHEW's health evaluation task force. We have not observed any definition of success measures that has met the tests of both external criticism and internal consensus.

b. FEDERAL EVALUATION POLICY

Part of the reason that individual evaluation offices have experienced difficulty in defining measurable success criteria is that no agreement exists within the total evaluation community on what evaluation office objectives should be and what success means. Each organization (OMB, GAO, Congress, and the individual agency evaluation offices) assumes its objectives and criteria, rarely documented, when it plans, guides, manages, or critiques evaluation activities and outputs. One can say that federal policies do exist at any given point in time by virtue of guidances from the Office of the Secretary, individual plans, position papers from OMB, and assessments of evaluation. The problem is that they all differ. There is, in fact, a continuing debate concerning the issue of evaluation objectives and success criteria; however, the debate over evaluation has not yet reached the stage at which individuals consciously recognize that they are in a policy debate which is conceptually similar to the policy debates that occur in the programmatic arena. In policy debates over programmatic issues (Should there be National Health Insurance? Should the Community Mental Health Center (CMHC) program be extended?) it is at least clear that a debate is taking place, even though common criteria may not always be used to influence or make decisions. So long as the debate continues without any common framework, evaluation offices will continue to face criticism from organizations and individuals who adopt different (and often changing) objectives and criteria of success.

B. PRIOR SOLUTIONS HAVE NOT WORKED

Many attempts have been made to improve evaluation--to make it more productive. We highlight a few of the solutions attempted in DHEW and examine briefly why they have not worked.

1. *EXAMPLES OF PRIOR SOLUTIONS*
    a. THE ORGANIZATION APPROACH

The former Assistant Secretary for Planning and Evaluation, under DHEW Secretary Robert Finch, decided that a central evaluation office at the Office of the Secretary would lead to more productive use of evaluation resources. No longer in the government, he has recently been quoted as recommending, on a more ambitious scale, the creation of a Federal Program Evaluation Office. "In order to overcome the many inadequacies of current program evaluation practices, he proposed the creation of a Federal Program Evaluation Office in either the Office of Management and Budget or in the Executive Office of the President to '[supervise] the evaluation activities of federal program agencies, [to conduct] a program of research on evaluation methods, and [to produce] an annual evaluation report'."[4]

To implement the earlier decision of ASPE, a strategy was adopted by the Office of the Secretary to: (1) develop and coordinate a department evaluation plan, (2) review and approve agency evaluation plans, and (3) conduct studies "to assure the timely availability of evaluation information for [feedback into the planning process affecting both resource allocation and program change]."[5] Of the total evaluation funds authorized by DHEW, the Office of the Secretary would retain control of 25 percent; roughly 50 percent were to be used by program management staffs, "Mostly to monitor the progress of the projects undertaken to achieve program goals;"[6] and the remaining 25 percent were to be used by agency offices of program planning and evaluation for broader types of evaluation. It was assumed that ASPE could influence agency evaluation programs so as to ensure "the timely availability of information" required by policy planners. "As a consequence of this negotiating leverage [review of plans and retention of 25 percent of the evaluation funds], evaluation projects are

---

4. Congressional Research Service, "Program Evaluation: Emerging Issues," November 16, 1974.
5. Laurence E. Lynn, Jr. "Notes from HEW," *Evaluation,* Fall 1972.
6. *Ibid.*

modified in the planning stage, often eliminating the need for independent OASPE projects. As a result of these economies, OASPE returns to the agencies a large portion of the monies set aside for the use of the Office of the Secretary and the OASPE."[7]

Has the ASPE approach resolved the problems? We note that critics of evaluation continue to charge that "the timely availability of evaluation information" for policy making has not been achieved. Our study of agency evaluation planning suggests that, despite ASPE review of plans and individual projects, agency plans continue to conform to agency needs and their content is barely affected by additional supervision. What has happened is that (1) agencies control only 75 percent of the funds available and what is left of the remaining 25 percent is often returned so late that they have difficulty in planning for its use;[8] (2) the process of defining an evaluation plan and having it approved consumes half the plan year; and (3) evaluation offices have been unable to anticipate ASPE review criteria, which have been *ad hoc*. We believe, then, that the ASPE policy has not worked because it did not incorporate activities and defined criteria that would allow ASPE to assess the success of agency evaluation objectives, plans, and projects.

b. THE PROGRAM APPROACH

Simultaneously, ASPE and others have attempted to implement approaches that have focused on making evaluation useful to program managers--in each case their unit of analysis was the "program."

The FY 1973 ASPE guidance defined program evaluation as: "The systematic assessment of existing programs and/or programmatic activities (including their development, scope and impact) for the extent to which they: (1) achieve their established objectives; (2) constitute the best alternative means of achieving these objectives; and (3) achieve those objectives in the most efficient manner possible." ASPE stated, "[Evaluation Study Project selection] has traditionally been on an eclectic, almost haphazard basis. The consequence has been a surfeit of data on some programs and none on others." The ASPE strategy was to force agencies to develop a matrix in which programs and available data were arranged according to effectiveness, alternatives, efficiency, and control. A strategic

---
7. *Ibid.*
8. *1974 Evaluation Plan for Health:* (Guidance from the Office of the Assistant Secretary for Health). "In 1973, P returned $3.5 million to HSMHA [Health Services and Mental Health Administration] from its 25 percent, more than half of which was returned in the last week of the fiscal year."

plan was to be developed by each agency to acquire data over a five-year period
that would fill data gaps. ASPE's guidance made certain assumptions:

- program objectives were defined;
- there was agreement on what constituted the definition of a pro-program;
- the information categories defined by ASPE were well enough defined to determine in which category studies would fall;
- the information categories represented the complete set of evaluation information required; and
- control over the mix and type of studies funded could be achieved using the information categories.

These assumptions all proved to be invalid: agencies completed their plans to match the ASPE format, but in the final analysis they defined projects as they always had, virtually without reference to ASPE guidance. Moreover, ASPE found it had no criteria for reviewing proposed evaluation study projects other than the traditional method--judgment on each evaluation project.

The NIMH Evaluation Branch, working with The Urban Institute during this same planning period, embarked on an experimental approach. After attempting to follow the ASPE guidance, NIMH recognized that it lacked well-defined program objectives. However, NIMH did want to focus evaluation resources on one subject--program evaluation. Working jointly, the Evaluation Branch and The Urban Institute team developed a draft evaluation policy specifying that evaluation resources would be used primarily for evaluation of the impact, effectiveness, and efficiency of *national* programs. The policy contained certain preconditions for evaluation: it required explicit statements of program objectives, measures of achievement, statements of hypotheses linking program activities to objectives, *and* a defined management use for the information. "Assessments of program evaluability"[9] were conducted by The Urban Institute team and the Evaluation Branch to assess the extent to which a number of NIMH's programs satisfied the preconditions. The intent was to define evaluation studies on the basis of these evaluability assessments.

The NIMH experiment was terminated because there was disagreement within NIMH generally and even within the Office of Program Planning and Evaluation on how evaluation funds should be used and who should decide their use. The

---

9. Examples of evaluability assessments conducted are contained in *Evaluation Planning at the National Institute of Mental Health: A Case History* by Pamela Horst, John W. Scanlon, Richard E. Schmidt, and Joseph S. Wholey, Paper 962-13, Washington, D.C., The Urban Institute, 1974.

disagreement led to circumvention of the draft evaluation policy and its eventual rejection.

2. *WHY PRIOR SOLUTIONS HAVE NOT WORKED*

There is general agreement that the approaches described above have failed, but no unanimity on the reasons for failure. Nevertheless, speculation about the possible causes would be useful in laying the foundations for a more successful approach.

Most importantly, we believe that prior approaches failed to define what was expected of evaluation offices. Both proponents and critics of evaluation use words like "utility" without ever defining what they mean. ASPE's guidance in FY 1973 turned into a writing exercise in which evaluation offices simply justified what they wanted to do anyway using definitions and terminology compatible with the ASPE policy. The similar terminology thus merely camouflaged the signs by which the success or failure of an evaluation office could have been known. Whatever kind of activity, product, or effect is desired, those who plan, manage, and review evaluation efforts must firmly agree on the evidence needed to demonstrate success. Without such agreement, any policy or guidance is liable to fail.

In part, however, failure can also be attributed to an inadequate concentration of staff working exclusively on evaluation. All approaches demand some minimum commitment of staff: the ASPE organization approach stressed the need to create pools of professional evaluators at several levels; both the ASPE program evaluation strategy and the NIMH/Urban Institute program evaluation approach implied the need (not well articulated in either case) for central control and planning within the evaluation offices. Yet, in reality, few evaluation offices in the health area have more than one or two evaluators and even these few divide their time between evaluation and other subjects. Many required activities cannot be performed simply because the available staff is too small. To the extent that adequate staff is not available, few approaches will work.

III. A DIFFERENT APPROACH

In view of the persistent problems and frequent failures that beset federal evaluation efforts, we must rethink the purposes and processes of evaluation and seriously consider a different approach. This and the subsequent chapters are devoted to the exposition of such an approach and its policy implications. Here we first review the thinking that led us to the metaphors of the marketplace in trying to construct a rational system for measuring success.

As we noted earlier, evaluation offices do have objectives, whether explicit or implicit, but they have rarely documented ways of measuring the degree of success in attaining objectives. We believe that success measures can be defined to match the objectives which the evaluation offices define.

A. COMMODITIES AND NEEDS

Evaluation offices view evaluation information as a commodity and the role of the evaluation office as serving that commodity to a variety of groups. By implication, then, we have "markets" for evaluation information, and we should try to define those markets. Such definitions are not easily arrived at, if we insist that they avoid the artificiality of prior definitions which incorporated standardized and unrealistic constructs of the way government actually operates.

In the next chapter, we define and explore the characteristics of three evaluation markets: (a) Individual Consumer Market, (b) Program Management Market, and (c) Policy Market. We have arrived at these market definitions by observing what evaluation offices actually do, what they say they want to do, what critics imply they ought to do, and by reviewing the subjects of debate in DHEW planning processes. We recognize that our use of a market analogy is an inexact translation from the business world and we do not imply that the federal government should adopt commercial methods of operation. We have used the analogy because it helped us to understand evaluation objectives and success criteria.

The *Individual Consumer Market* seemed a natural characterization of the group of federal government individuals and organizations who demand studies or funds to support studies to help them carry out their individual missions or tasks. There appear to be several reasons why this evaluation market exists and places a demand on evaluation resources. We know that the job of government, especially in the area of social programs, involves working with an immense number of unknowns. Individuals are constantly being asked to adopt or support some position about which they feel the need for more information. Secondly, much of DHEW's mission has a research character, either explicitly or implicitly. Each piece of acquired information opens a new question, suggesting yet another study. Additionally, many managers believe that a particular activity (a seminar, for example) would be worth conducting because it would help them accomplish their mission. For many of these types of studies and activities, there are few available sources of funds, one of the few being the funds established under Section 513 of the Public Health Service Act (the so-called 1 percent evaluation set-aside). Despite the definitional schemes established in evaluation guidances, what constitutes an "acceptable" category of studies for 1 percent funding is so ambiguous that the evaluation money is virtually unrestricted.[1] Hence a market which we term the Individual Consumer Market.

The *Program Management Market* is quite different. Neither The Urban Institute team nor the majority of evaluation offices has been able to identify a well-articulated demand for performance information from program managers. However, several pieces of evidence suggest that there is at least an intended market. First, the legislative language authorizing evaluation funds suggests that evaluation of programs is intended (as distinct, say, from research). Second, as Secretary Finch said in 1969 in his testimony before the House Committee on Education and Labor:

> *Evaluation is a necessary foundation for effective implementation and judicious modification of our existing programs. At this point evaluation is probably more important than the addition of new laws to an already extensive list of educational statutes. . . . Evaluation will provide the information we require to strengthen weak programs, fully support effective programs, and drop those which simply are not fulfilling the objectives intended by the Congress when the programs were originally enacted.*

The intention clearly stated by Secretary Finch at the beginning of the "evaluation era" was to make major programmatic changes, as appropriate, based on

---
1. A relatively recent definition of *evaluation* adopted by the DHEW health evaluation task force illustrates the broad interpretation of evaluation in the context of the 1 percent funding. See Appendix C.

evaluation results. Evaluation seems to be described here as the study of existing programs to determine the extent to which they are achieving *congressional objectives,* with the purpose of supporting, modifying, or eliminating programs depending on the outcome. Finally, many evaluation offices (e.g., NIMH in 1973 and 1974) have explicitly defined their objectives in terms of serving the needs of program management. Through statements of intent, then, we see a potential second market, Program Management whose demand can be verified by attempting to serve the market.

Our third market, the Policy Market, is also a *potential* market, not because policy debates do not take place, but because the authors of this report (and many federal evaluators) are not sure to what extent such debates can be enlightened by evaluation studies. A "policy" is a particulary elusive term to define in the abstract. We know that policy debates take place, sometimes formally within the context of DHEW's planning processes such as forward planning and budgeting and sometimes informally. Yet neither the subjects of the debates nor the actors involved lend themselves to a usable definition. Policy issues cover many subjects and, even though programs are involved, the achievement of program objectives *per se* need not be the focal point of the debate. An essential characteristic might be that policy issues are questions of some type which concern what the government should be doing and which are being debated across a number of organizational lines (DHEW vs. OMB, ASPE vs. ASH, and ADAMHA vs. ASH) or across the bounds of a single agency (NIMH). Clearly the debate over the most appropriate form of National Health Insurance is a recognizable policy issue. Through examination of DHEW's forward planning,[2] its Operational Planning System,[3] and its budget process,[4] it was apparent many policy issues were being debated, even though the formal documents (forward plans, etc.) often provided only scant information about the nature of the debate, the participants, or the substance of the arguments. ASH's approach to forward planning during the FY 1975 planning process and its approach to evaluation planning during FY 1973 both suggest that "issues" need to be defined

---

2. Pamela Horst, John W. Scanlon and Richard E. Schmidt. "The Forward Plan, Problems and Possibilities for an Effective Alcohol, Drug Abuse and Mental Health Administration Role," Washington, D.C., The Urban Institute, November 1974.

3. Pamela Horst, John W. Scanlon and Richard E. Schmidt. "The Operational Planning System," Washington, D.C., The Urban Institute, March 13, 1975.

4. Pamela Horst, John W. Scanlon and Richard E. Schmidt. "Observations on the Department of Health, Education, and Welfare Budget Process," Washington, D.C., The Urban Institute, March 27, 1975 [in draft].

and debated, although ASH never operationally defines what it means by an "issue." We believe that an abstract definition of "policy" would introduce more problems (semantic ones, if nothing else) than it would resolve. We approach the question from the premise that planners and managers within DHEW could, within reasonable limits, sit together in a room and define most of the important "policy issues" being debated within their area of interest, even if they could not define accurately all of the participants, what the participants believe, and why they hold those beliefs. We know, as we have said above, that there is considerable discussion among planners and evaluators as to whether or not such policy debates could be facilitated or enlightened through evaluation, but there is also criticism of the minor role which evaluation plays in such debates. These observations, then, led us to define a third evaluation market--the *Policy Market*.

Chapter IV explores the characteristics of these markets in detail. Chapter V examines alternative approaches that can be used by evaluation offices to serve one or more of these markets. A key part of these suggested approaches is that the evaluation office imposes no artificial models of how decision makers or programs function. Rather, the evaluation offices permit the individuals and organizations in each market to define their missions in their own terms. This removes one barrier that currently seems to inhibit evaluation offices from serving real management functions as distinct from rhetorical or idealized statements of those functions. Another major element of the suggested approaches is that we add an enlarged and routine activity to be conducted by evaluation office--the measurement of its success in serving each market.

In the foregoing discussion we have focused on the federal markets served by federal evaluation offices, although we recognize that other markets exist. The most important of these are state and local units of government, and individual project managers in the field. Although a few evaluation offices at the federal level in DHEW include some of these organizations as users, by far the greatest activity and the vast majority of outputs are directed towards federal users at the headquarters level. The Urban Institute has worked with other federal agencies attempting to serve state and local governments and we have worked with such government units directly. A substantial amount of our work with the Law Enforcement Assistance Administration (LEAA), for example, is concerned with providing evaluation information as well as self-evaluation capability to state and local government units.[5] Our experience suggests that the subject—how federal evaluation offices can provide evaluation information to help state and local governments—is substantial in its own right and could not be treated adequately within this report.

B. WHY DOES THE SUGGESTED APPROACH PROMISE TO RESOLVE THE PROBLEMS WHERE OTHERS HAVE FAILED?

The approach that we define in subsequent chapters recognizes that prior approaches to evaluation management and control have run into difficulty because they failed to establish agreement on objectives and on the type and level of evidence needed to demonstrate success. Our approach includes the following ingredients.

1. *SUCCESS CRITERIA FOR EVALUATION OFFICES SUGGESTED*

We illustrate evaluation office success criteria for each market and define different levels of evidence that can be used to prove to evaluation office management and others that the evaluation office is meeting its objectives.

The objectives and success criteria to use in managing or critiquing an evaluation office were selected to meet the following requirements:

- A strong causal connection can be made between the success criteria and the evaluation office activities.
- The evaluation office can be held directly responsible for achieving the objective.
- The success criteria are defined as measures of "market" use or response to the evaluation product.

We believe that some criteria should not be used to measure evaluation office performance. For example, "producing an increase in program performance," while being a desirable end, is beyond the direct responsibility of the evaluation office in that its achievement depends upon management actions. While this may be an interesting research question to explore (i.e., does evaluation result in an increase in performance), we believe it is an inappropriate success measure for management of evaluation.

---

5. The Urban Institute is assisting LEAA's National Institute of Law Enforcement and Criminal Justice to implement its National Evaluation Program, a program designed to serve local as well as certain federal needs. (See Nay et al., "Work Description for a Phase I Study for the National Evaluation Program.") The Institute has also completed a series of Prescriptive Packages—studies that summarize local experience with such activities as evaluation systems, monitoring systems, burglary prevention, team policing, civilians in police work, and criminal investigation.

In the approach, we suggest that the final judgment of levels of evidence be left to evaluation office managers, who must decide to whom they are accountable. We note that evaluation offices require evidence both to guide their own activities and to account to others for their actions (often to defend themselves against criticism). We believe the latter need to be important, although we also believe that evaluation offices must decide for themselves how important it is (and, therefore, what level of evidence is needed) to fend off criticism and justify their programs.

The success criteria perform another related function; they establish a common basis for reviewing success--measures that at least permit different groups, planners, reviewers, and evaluators to argue on the same basis.

2. *NO ARBITRARY MODELS OF THE DECISION-MAKING PROCESS ARE DEFINED*

Models of programs, decision processes, individual behavior, etc., often serve a useful purpose--they permit planners to reduce complex situations to key elements, thus focusing their attention on what is most important. But when the models do not accurately represent reality, they fail to assist planners. We are not talking of models that are overly simplistic but of models that often represent a world different from the one that exists. In our approach we try to avoid artificial constructs or models which imply methods of government operation that simply do not exist. Three federal markets for evaluation are distinguished--but *no* models describing how decisions are reached and what information decision makers need are prescribed. Instead, within a market, the evaluation office relies on agencies to define their own "programs" and "policy issues."

3. *MARKET DEMAND STUDIES ARE SUGGESTED*

What is the demand in each market? Evaluation offices already know what the demand is in one of the three markets--the Individual Consumer Market. Neither they nor we know the extent of demand from policy makers or program managers. This report does not resolve the question, but it does suggest a method by which it can be resolved. We suggest the need to systematically test the demand in these two markets to determine whether it exists in a form that can be served by evaluation offices. The question is germane, since the debate and much of the criticism imply that evaluation fails to respond to the needs in the market.

4. *RECOMMENDATIONS ARE MADE TO DEVELOP A FEDERAL EVALUATION POLICY*

The absence of any clear federal evaluation policy that specifies what is expected of evaluation offices and what evidence is acceptable to demonstrate success makes it difficult to plan, manage, and review evaluation. It is no less a policy issue than are debates over what ought to be the objectives of a social program. There are two parts to the debate: (a) What do policy makers *believe* should be accomplished by evaluation offices? (b) What can evaluation offices actually accomplish? We suggest in the final chapter that this issue should be addressed as a major policy issue and that it should be the focus of a study which uses the "market" approach as a method of resolution.

IV. THE THREE FEDERAL MARKETS FOR EVALUATION INFORMATION

A. INTRODUCTION

As previously suggested, it has been our experience that evaluation offices, for the most part, attempt to serve three types of federal markets. The three markets are defined in terms of federal organizational units and individuals carrying out some common function or task. Each market will have a number of potential customers for evaluation information.

- A customer in the Individual Consumer Market is defined as an individual federal government employee carrying out his mission in the manner he chooses.

- A customer in the Program Management Market is defined as the set of organizational managers responsible for implementing a specific program and overseeing its implementation.

- A customer in the Policy Market is defined as the set of organizational managers involved in debating and resolving a specific issue over policy; i.e., what the government will do.

Each market represents a different objective from the viewpoint of the evaluation office.

In the Individual Consumer Market, the evaluation office sees a group of federal government employees involved in various tasks or missions. The evaluation office tries to help each individual by providing information tailored to what the individual thinks he needs to do his job.

In the Program Management Market, the evaluation office sees a number of organizational units with some role in implementing or overseeing federal program activities in order to accomplish program objectives. The evaluation office attempts to aid implementation by providing feedback on how well program activities are being implemented and how well objectives are being met. Here the information is tailored to program management definitions of objectives and activities.

In the Policy Market, the evaluation office sees a large number of organizational units with some role in influencing or resolving an issue. The evaluation office attempts to clarify that debate by providing information on which those involved in it can more soundly base their opinions and positions.

This chapter examines each market to identify its characteristics and to describe the objectives and success criteria for an evaluation office serving it.

B. THE INDIVIDUAL CONSUMER MARKET

1. *WHAT IS THE MISSION OF INDIVIDUAL CONSUMERS?*

An evaluation office sees many potential consumers for its product. For example, in DHEW an evaluation office at the institute level sees the following:

- congressional committees,
- Executive Office of the President,
- Office of the Secretary,
- Office of the Assistant Secretary for Health,
- ADAMHA Administrator,
- Institute Directors,
- planning staff groups at each level,
- program directors within the institute, and
- program office staff at each level.

Collectively, the job these potential consumer groups carry out is running a large part of the government. They decide what the government is going to do and how it will do it, and then they carry through the implementation of programs and policies. Everyone acknowledges that the process through which these missions are carried out and the rules governing this process are complex and do not lend themselves to simple modeling.

If the evaluation office is to develop evaluation information of some utility to the government process, it has to produce information which aids the potential customers in carrying out their mission. But we know that:

- the missions are defined by the participants;
- the groups listed have several missions; and
- the missions are not carried out according to any well-defined set of procedures, decision rules, and schedules.

All this is to say that an evaluation office has difficulty in knowing how to affect the government process through its evaluation program. It is not clear:

- what it means to affect the government process (how is information "utility" defined);
- who the participants are whose needs should be served; and
- what the information needs are.

In principle, if the evaluation office were to assess the ultimate utility of its product, it would have to know how each consumer carried out his mission and how that mission was affected by the information. Some model of the individual's mission would be necessary to define evaluation impact. (In fact, this is what the evaluation office attempts to do in the policy and program management markets.) However, evaluation offices frequently conclude that since the number of individual missions is so great[1] and their interrelationships so little known,[2] it is practically impossible to trace the impact of information on government process. It is assumed that each individual through his definition of his job and his experience in carrying it out has to determine what evaluation information is needed, how he will use it, and when it is useful.

2. *WHO ARE THE CONSUMERS?*

A consumer in the Individual Consumer Market is defined as a federal government employee carrying out his mission in the manner he chooses. This market includes every individual who asks an evaluation office to provide funds for a study that the individual considers necessary or useful to his work. Different consumers need studies for a variety of reasons. The following kinds of requests are typical:

- A branch or division manager needs assistance in analyzing data from a monitoring system.
- A division manager wants to study the extent and causes of unequal manpower distribution.
- A branch manager wants assistance in planning his research program.
- A researcher wants information on the negative side-effects of psychotherapy.
- An evaluator in the Office of the Secretary wants to know the potential impact on local schools in a particular city if court-enforced integration is imposed.
- An agency administrator wants to know why doctors join and stay in the Public Health Service.

The studies are funded in response to demands placed on the evaluation office, and the nature of the study is dictated by the needs of the consumer as

---

1. Missions can range from providing technical assistance to grantees to negotiating policy with OMB and Congress; from doing research to funding researchers.
2. Except at the highest policy and management levels, the actions of any *one* individual do not usually have a significant impact on the government process.

perceived by the consumer. An evaluation office can be set up to serve a variety of individual consumers in an agency or just one consumer.

3. *OBJECTIVES AND SUCCESS CRITERIA FOR THE EVALUATION OFFICE SERVING THE INDIVIDUAL CONSUMER MARKET*

The objective of the evaluation office in this market is to provide the information that meets the individual consumers' needs as perceived by the consumers.

The evaluation office serving the Individual Consumer Market operates under a series of assumptions, such as:

- if a requested study is produced according to specifications, a particular customer will review it (the request may be formal or informal); and
- if the customer reviews it, the information will meet that customer's perceived needs.

Each of these assumptions can be tested by the evaluation office once the study is available.

The measure of how effectively the evaluation office serves the market should include customer satisfaction with the product. Study completion alone is not an adequate success measure. Moreover, whether or not the *customer* effectively uses the information to do his job better is *not* a measure of evaluation office success in serving the Individual Consumer Market. For example, if the consumer wants a policy-oriented or program management study, what is the measure of success for the evaluation office? Our answer is that it depends on how the evaluation office views its responsibilities. If the intent of the evaluation office is to produce a study satisfactory to a consumer, then the office is serving the Individual Consumer Market. The responsibility for taking the necessary steps to actually affect policy or program management is in the hands of the consumer, not the evaluation office. The evaluation office accepts responsibility only for producing a study to specifications defined by the consumer. (In practice, it may accept even less responsibility, providing only funding and playing only a minor role in contract administration.) Should the study produced to consumer specifications fail to affect policy or program management, then the evaluation office has achieved its objectives, but the consumer has not.

When it comes to measuring success in this market, the evaluation office can rely on three levels of evidence (reflecting different degrees of confidence):

I. The opinion of the *evaluation office* that the customer was satisfied based on informal discussions with the customer.

II. The documented opinion of *consumers* who have had an opportunity to review and react to the final product.

III. Measurement of consumer satisfaction by comparing customer needs and expectations taken prior to dissemination of the final product with customer reaction and opinion after dissemination.

The first type of evidence, based on discussions with customers or feedback through informal channels, may be valuable to the evaluator, but it does not produce a success measure which an outside reviewer would consider objective and have confidence in. The second and third types are more direct measures of the evaluation office objective and produce evidence in which a reviewer can place higher confidence.

The decision whether to rely on informal or formal customer opinion surveys will depend in part on how necessary it is for the evaluation office to account for its performance to agency directors and outside groups.

Whatever decision is made, for management purposes, evaluation offices should consult consumers after they have had an opportunity to review and react to the final product. It is to be anticipated that individual consumers will not be uniformly satisfied. (At a minimum, they should all receive a product.) In striving to be successful, the evaluation office should attempt to define the reasons for successful and unsuccessful studies. Bearing in mind that there are no uniform criteria to be applied--each study will reflect the extent to which contractor and consumer understand the nature of the product desired. The evaluation office should determine whether:

- the product is faulty technically;
- the product is of acceptable quality, but the consumer disagrees with the findings and conclusions;
- the product is of acceptable quality, but the subject is not germane to the consumer's needs; or
- the product arrived too late to be of any value.

Separating these issues is complex and often, given the nature of both RFPs and contracts, there are no fixed scientific standards that can be applied. The purpose of conducting such a survey, however, is to improve the probability of successful evaluation studies in the future. If, for example, the product is considered technically inadequate, the evaluation office needs to determine whether the task was infeasible or the contractor's staff was incompetent. If the product itself seems to be technically acceptable (on judgmental grounds) but the consumer disagrees with the results, then the fault may well lie with the consumer's original expectations, or a failure in communication between the evaluator and consumer.

Repeated surveys of the type described will increase the ability of the evaluation office to screen evaluation proposals, prepare and review RFPs, and monitor contracts. In short, evaluation and feedback of its own program should enable the office to function more effectively to satisfy the consumers in this market.

C. THE PROGRAM MANAGEMENT MARKET

1. *WHAT IS A PROGRAM?*

One mission of an agency is managing a set of programs to achieve a set of objectives. In the federal government, the term "program" typically refers to a set of related federal activities and resources that are brought together to achieve common objectives of national scope. An evaluation office frequently defines its mission as evaluating agency programs to support the management of those programs. An evaluation office attempting to serve program management frequently runs into two problems: (a) what constitutes a program is not always clear to the evaluation office, and (b) program designs, in which measurable objectives are linked to program activities in some testable way, have not been established by management.

While the definition of programs may appear straightforward, it can be a confusing task to the evaluation office acting on its own. There are several sources of conflicting definitions. The legislation prescribes one set of activities and objectives, the organizational structure may prescribe a second set (is a program what an organizational unit does?) and the budget structure may imply yet another. For example, it is not clear whether NIMH's CMHC program (administered by the Mental Health Services Division) is separate and distinct from Mental Health Services Research (administered by a branch within the division). Is it one program, of which research is a component, providing support to the centers,[3] or are there two separate programs?

---

3. See *Evaluation Planning at the National Institute of Mental Health: A Case History* (Pamela Horst, John W. Scanlon, Richard E. Schmidt and Joseph S. Wholey), The Urban Institute, 1974, Chapter V for examples of the ambiguity that arises in an agency when one attempts to define programs for evaluation.

Thus, the legislation may authorize a number of activities which can be considered either parts of one program or individual programs in themselves. Moreover, an organization usually manages a number of "internal programs" (activities and outputs of federal staff) which are distinct from "external programs" (the group of activities or projects funded in the field, for example, the CMHCs). For this market, the evaluation office assumes that it cannot arbitrarily define what is and what is not a program. The only useful approach open to the evaluation office is to have the agency itself define what its major programs are.

A program design refers to the specification of program objectives, program activities, and the assumptions which link accomplishment of activities to achievement of objectives. Evaluation offices too often find that a program has no objectives stated in measurable terms and no linking assumptions articulated that can be empirically tested. Further investigation often finds management in disagreement over objectives or unwilling to specify measurable objectives.

Traditionally, when evaluation offices decide to conduct an evaluation under these conditions, they defined the absence of objectives as a methodological problem. In that case they undertake method development or perform the evaluation with measures specified by the evaluator (the contractor). Such efforts have had little use to program management for a number of reasons: (1) they have defined a program different from management's perception of the program, (2) management does not understand the methodology, (3) management finds itself unable to act upon the results, and (4) such studies are notorious for being inconclusive.

In serving the Program Management Market, the evaluation office will assume that specification of the program design is the responsibility of management (and perhaps a policy issue arises because of disagreement). Line management should define the activities that constitute the program and the objectives of the program. The evaluation office will work with program management to extract their program design and use that design as a basis for evaluating the program. We will discuss in Chapter V the technique of "evaluability assessment" that was developed in earlier Urban Institute work with NIMH for the purpose of reaching agreement with management on a program design statement.

2. *WHO IS THE CUSTOMER?*

Customers in the Program Management Market are the set of managers responsible for (a) applying program resources and carrying out activities to meet a program's objectives, and (b) overseeing implementation of that program. The customer in this market carries out the following types of activities:

- *program design*--specifying the organization and nature of program activity in the field, federal staff activities, resource requirements, and the regulations and guidelines governing the program;
- *program resource allocation*--distributing program funds and staff to federal staff activities and individual projects, contracts, and grants; and
- *oversight and direction of the program*--the supervision, review, technical advice, policy interpretation given to program staff by managers and policy makers.

For a specific program, an evaluation office might have to consider program management as including congressional committees, OMB, and the Office of the Secretary, as well as the institute director and program division manager. We now call them part of program management because they are fulfilling certain types of roles with respect to the program. For a given program, however, the cast of program management changes over time. For example, at the time of legislative renewal, Congress, the Executive Office of the President, and the Office of the Secretary temporarily function as program managers by renewing or revising the legislation which provides the initial definition of the program design. Similarly, at budget hearings, these groups assume a program management role by allocating resources to program activities. At other times and for different kinds of decisions, these groups usually are not involved and thus the program management group becomes synonymous with institute management.

An evaluation office working on the CMHC program might consider the following people as potential customers in the Program Management Market:

- Director Mental Health Services Division,
- Director National Institute of Mental Health,
- Administrator, Alcohol, Drug Abuse and Mental Health Administration, and
- Budget Examiner, Office of Management and Budget.

The evaluation office will attempt to provide this group with the information that the group collectively thinks it needs to manage the program (including resource allocation as a management function) to meet its objectives.

evaluation office frequently identifies policy makers and policy issues as important targets for evaluation information.

"Policy" is a decision about what government will do. A policy issue is a controversy, disagreement, or debate over some course of action. Such issues may take many forms:

- *What is our policy toward service programs?* Should the federal government be funding direct health services, or is that a function of state and local government?
- *Should a new program be established?* Should the administration support National Health Insurance?
- *What should be the objective of a program?* Should research money be spent on applied research or basic research?
- *Does a current program represent our new policies?* Should federal support for the CMHC program be discontinued given the administration's policy of encouraging states to assume responsibility for service programs?

Policy defines or conveys the fundamental principles by which government will or will not intervene in society. Policies may range in size (budget level) from decisions to push National Health Insurance to decisions that would eliminate federal support for pre-doctoral training. Policy made at one level of government (Executive Office) often entails the modification or resulution of policy issues at lower levels of government (e.g., a debate between the OS and ADAMHA over discontinuation of the CMHC program).

A great many decisions are made in running the government, most of which will probably not affect the Policy Market. How does an evaluation office distinguish a policy-related issue from some other type? Content and subject matter do not always distinguish policy issues from other issues. (For example, it is a mistake to arbitrarily characterize the question "What is the impact of program X on the target group?" as a policy issue, and the question "What is the cost-effectiveness of program X?" as a program management issue.) A policy issue is, by definition, a *debate* which is carried out between organizational units in some position to influence or decide what the objectives of an agency are and how the agency will achieve those objectives. The evaluation office must then define what policy issues government policy makers are actually debating. Frequently, a policy issue centers on the question of cost-effectiveness or, for that matter, on the political practicality of getting consensus on an approach. The content of a policy issue and the basis for its resolution will vary from issue to issue.

2. *WHO IS THE CUSTOMER?*

A customer in the Policy Market is defined as the set of decision makers involved in debating and resolving a specific issue over what the government will do.

The evaluation office assumes that a number of people will influence the final policy decisions and that a smaller number of people will have a direct hand in making the final decision. Each of these actors will bring different political philosophies, opinions, perceptions, and positions to the policy debate. It is probably impossible to weigh with any accuracy the influence or impact different actors have on the policy-making process. The evaluation office assumes that it will often be difficult, and in some cases impractical, to determine who made certain policy decisions and what information influenced that decision. Therefore, the evaluation office attempts to influence the collective opinion and attitudes of those involved in the debate.

Since people in a large number of organizational units may be involved in one debate, it may be difficult to sort out arguments and positions. A convenient device to use in defining a customer in the Policy Market is that of an interface. An interface consists of two groups involved in some decision-making process involving a debate over what policy should be, or how policy should be implemented. Some of these interfaces may be *ad hoc*--such as between agency administrators and congressional committees during a debate on a particular piece of legislation--or formal--such as between OMB and DHEW during the annual budget process.

A customer is defined by *all the interfaces* involved in the debate over one issue. For example, the issue of whether or not to continue funding CMHCs might involve the following three interfaces: NIMH vs. OMB during the preparation of the budget; Congress vs. OMB during hearings on the renewal of legislation; NIMH vs. Congress during appropriation hearings.

3. *OBJECTIVES AND SUCCESS CRITERIA FOR THE EVALUATION OFFICE SERVING THE POLICY MARKET*

The objective of the evaluation office in serving the Policy Market is to provide information which changes (or strengthens) the opinions, attitudes, and positions of those involved in a policy debate.

The evaluation office serving the Policy Market operates under such assumptions as:

- if information related to a specific issue is produced, the findings will be reviewed and considered by decision makers;
- if decision makers review the findings, a significant percentage of them will modify their attitudes and opinions; and
- if decision makers change their attitudes and opinions, a significant proportion will change or reinforce their positions on an issue.

Each of these assumptions can be tested once the evaluation study is available.

The success criteria for the evaluation office include changes in the attitudes and positions of those involved in the policy debate. The production of a study and the quality of the study are not, alone, adequate criteria for evaluation office success. On the other hand, the outcome of the debate is not a realistic success criterion. The evaluation office assumes it will *influence* outcome by affecting the collective attitude of decision makers. However, the outcome of a debate, if it can be tracked at all, will be influenced by a large number of factors other than evaluation. In any event, a necessary condition for establishing a causal relationship between evaluation and policy outcome would be to show that the collective attitude of the customer was affected by the evaluation.

In demonstrating success, the evaluation office can rely on several levels of evidence which differ in the degree of confidence an outside reviewer would have in that evidence:

I. The opinion of the evaluation office that the customer's opinions and attitudes were affected by the evaluation.

II. The documented opinion of the customer that the study was useful.

III. Measurement of changes in attitudes and opinions of a sample of targeted decision makers taken by survey after dissemination of study findings.

IV. Measurement of changes in attitudes and opinions of a sample of targeted decision makers by survey before *and* after dissemination of study findings.

The first two types of subjective evidence may be useful to evaluation office management, but it is likely that an outside reviewer would not find them persuasive.

The third and fourth types are more direct tests of the assumptions under which the evaluation office operates. In these two cases, the collection of evidence includes an opinion survey organized around a strategy for disseminating the study results. Once the study results are known to the evaluation office, it can estimate how the findings will affect attitudes and which attitudes might be affected. This information can guide the development of structured opinion surveys to measure existing attitudes and changes in attitudes. The report can then be distributed in some form to decision makers and those who influence decision makers.

Whether it is practical and feasible to survey policy makers systematically so as to measure the impact of a study is not yet known.

E. COMPARISON OF THE OBJECTIVES AND SUCCESS CRITERIA FOR THE THREE MARKETS

Tables 1 and 2 summarize the discussion in this chapter. Table 1 gives the objectives and success criteria for an evaluation office serving each market, and Table 2 shows the levels of evidence that can be developed on evaluation office performance.

These two tables illustrate two very important points:
- different evaluation markets have different success criteria; and
- each market has different levels of evidence of performance which can be demanded by different reviewers.

Much of the criticism leveled at evaluation and the uncertainty in planning is related to these two points.

Frequently, agency evaluation offices are serving the Individual Consumer Market and assessing their own performance accordingly, while outside review groups (OMB, GAO, Office of the Secretary) often imply that they ought to be serving the Program Management and Policy Markets. Any study could be reviewed by a number of critics with each critic defining success differently because (1) each held different objectives and (2) each required different levels of evidence. There is usually no evidence available which outside reviewers would find persuasive for any market because the evaluation offices do not aggressively develop such evidence.

In the past, policy makers have attempted to set evaluation policy and direct evaluation efforts by such means as:
- classifying evaluation studies and calling for certain types of evaluation;
- establishing organizational arrangements to produce evaluation; and
- establishing elaborate planning requirements that have to be met before expenditure of evaluation funds are approved.

TABLE 1: OBJECTIVES AND SUCCESS CRITERIA FOR AN EVALUATION OFFICE

The Federal Market for Evaluation	The Objective of the Evaluation Office	Customers for the Evaluation Information	Evaluation Office Success Criteria
Individual Consumer Market	To provide information that satisfies the perceived needs of the individual consumer.	The individual federal employee carrying out his mission in the manner he chooses.	Customer satisfaction with the evaluation product.
Program Management Market	To provide information which program management acts upon to maintain or change a program design.	Those organizational managers responsible for implementing a program and overseeing the implementation of that program.	Action taken by management on evaluation results to affect the program design.
Policy Market	To provide information which changes the opinions, attitudes and positions of those involved in the policy debate.	Those organizational managers involved in debating and resolving a policy issue.	Changes in attitudes, opinions and positions as a result of the evaluation findings.

TABLE 2: LEVELS OF EVIDENCE FOR DIFFERENT USES ON EVALUATION OFFICE PERFORMANCE

The Federal Market for Evaluation	Types of Evidence Appropriate for Evaluation Office Management	Types of Evidence Persuasive to Outside Reviewers
Individual Consumer Market	I. The opinion of the evaluation office that the customer was satisfied, based on informal discussions with the customer.	II. The documented opinion of consumers who had an opportunity to review and react to the final product. III. Measurement of consumer satisfaction by comparing customer needs and expectations taken prior to dissemination of the final product with customer reaction and opinion after dissemination.
Program Management Market	I. The opinion of the evaluation office that the customer acted upon the information. II. The documented opinion of program management that information was useful and was acted upon.	III. Documentation of the action taken by program management to maintain or modify the program design based on evaluation findings.
Policy Market	I. The opinion of the evaluation office that the customer's opinions and attitudes were affected by the evaluation. II. The documented opinion of the customer that the study was useful.	III. Measurement of changes in attitudes and opinions of a sample of targeted decision makers by survey after dissemination of study findings. IV. Measurement of changes in attitudes and opinions of a sample of targeted decision makers by survey before *and* after dissemination of study findings.

All such efforts have failed to still the criticism or satisfy the evaluation policy makers. They failed because they ignored the central problem--evaluation policy has lacked objectives and specification of the level of evidence required to demonstrate performance. If an evaluation policy for actually governing evaluation offices is to be defined, it will be necessary to prescribe the type and level of evidence that the evaluation offices will be required to develop on each study.

V. SERVING A MARKET FOR FEDERAL EVALUATION

A. INTRODUCTION

Once an evaluation office has determined which market or markets it serves, it must plan those studies required, and see that they are executed and disseminated. Moreover, the evaluation office must be assured that it has the organizational capability to serve the market selected.

In this chapter, we examine the requirements imposed by the market on the evaluation office. We examine each market to determine how the evaluation office selects studies, what number and types of study are needed and the organizational requirements for operating the evaluation office.

B. THE INDIVIDUAL CONSUMER MARKET

1. *DEFINING THE INFORMATION NEEDED BY THE MARKET*

To serve the market, the evaluation office has to decide:
- what individual consumers it will serve; and
- what information those consumers need.

The first decision is frequently imposed on the evaluation office by line supervisors or is determined by staff and contract resources. For example, an Assisthat Secretary may set up an evaluation office solely to do studies of interest to him. In another case, a one- or two-person evaluation staff with a large contract budget may require the program offices to take the lead in defining and developing studies. An agency administrator may assume responsibility for the final choice of both customer's studies.

When the evaluation office has some discretion in choosing between customers and between evaluation projects, there is no single set of rules to follow in making the choise. An evaluation office might subjectively rank potential customers on how important the evaluation office thinks the customer's mission is, and on how great a contribution the evaluation project will make to that mission provided the evaluation project satisfies the customer's perceived needs. Any number of additional criteria might be considered, including the potential customer's political clout in the agency. The evaluation planning process will elicit suggested projects that individuals in this market want funded; i.e., *individuals* may act singly and alone or in some sort of conjunction with each other. When some choice of customers and projects has to be made, the decisions will be made on a judgmental basis by the evaluation office or by some line authority over the evaluation office.

A planning issue related to choice of customers is the degree to which the information needed by the customer must be specified--that is, how much interaction with the customer and how much analysis of proposed evaluation projects is necessary on the part of the evaluation office to assure success.

The success criterion for the Individual Consumer Market is the opinion of the consumer that the evaluation project met the needs he perceived for it. An evaluation office could ultimately fail by misreading the needs of the customer or by allowing the customer to have unrealistic expectations of what can be produced. Therefore, planning by the evaluation office can be viewed as an attempt to assure that the following conditions are met:

- the evaluation office understands what the customer's perceived needs are;
- the customer's needs can be met by the evaluation project selected; and
- the evaluation project is feasible to carry out.

On any one evaluation project, the evaluation office may find itself in one of the following situations:

- Informal discussions with the customer provide the necessary assurances. The evaluation office feels it has sufficient guidance to carry out an evaluation project which will satisfy the customer.
- Informal discussions with the customer do not provide the assurances. The evaluation office feels that it must clarify the evaluation requirements, change the customer's expectations and his perception of need, or test to make sure that the evaluation project is feasible.

The first situation comes up frequently and includes cases where the evaluation project requested is clear cut (e.g., a regression analysis of a particular program information system) and where the customer is looking for descriptive information on the status of a program or problem (such as a survey of field projects to determine their technical assistance requirements).

The second situation can occur in a number of ways. For example, a customer may want a study that supports his arguments on some issue while the evaluation office feels that such a study would counter his argument. If the evaluation office goes ahead and is correct, it will fail to meet the perceived needs of the customer. Once the evaluation office concludes that the customer's perceived needs are unreasonable or unrealistic, it must work with the customer to change those perceptions. A similar situation could occur if the study requested was methodologically infeasible. Many federal officials have expressed disappointment with evaluation studies because they tend to be inconclusive and methodologically weak. Here, evaluation offices may have failed to challenge and change the unrealistic expectations of individual consumers.

To increase the evaluation project's chances of satisfying the needs of the customer, there are two principal approaches available to the evaluation office--one organizational, one interactive.

Organizationally, the evaluation office can delegate the design of the project to the customer himself. If the customer has the time and capability, this is one effective way to assure that the needs of the customer are correctly defined. Frequently though, the customer will not be able to assume this role and will rely on the evaluation office to help design and develop evaluation projects. In this situation, the evaluation office would have to consider undertaking a more systematic analysis of the customer's needs.

In the interactive approach, the evaluation office carries out two tasks: (a) analyzing the customer's statement of need for evaluation, and (b) interacting with the customer to reach agreement on the kind of evaluation project needed and on reasonable expectations for that project. Since there is no set of rules and procedures for carrying out these tasks that will assure success, the amount and type of analysis and interaction will vary from case to case.[1]

To summarize, then, an evaluation office serving the Individual Consumer Market must administer a planning process which selects customers to be served and develops their evaluation needs in sufficient detail for the evaluation office to have some assurance of success. What constitutes sufficient detail and sufficient assurance of success are judgments made by the evaluation office. The evaluation office objective and success criteria in the Individual Consumer Market imply that the evaluation office will have to reach some mutual agreement with the customer on what are reasonable expectations for the evaluation

---

1. One approach to analysis of the customer's evaluation requirements is outlined in "Urban Institute Plan for the Design of an Evaluation" by John Waller and John Scanlon, Washington, D. C., The Urban Institute, 1973.

project in order to have assurance of success in the end. The range of planning approaches available to the evaluation office is illustrated by the following options:

- The evaluation office can select customers and then allow them to develop their own evaluation projects.
- The evaluation office can work with potential customers to develop their projects and then select customers on the basis of expected success in meeting their needs.
- The evaluation office can select customers and then simply guess what evaluation projects they will need, not bothering to interact or reach agreement with the customer.

Each has different organizational and workload requirements for an evaluation office, as discussed in Section 3 below.

2. *SERVING THE MARKET: THE LEVEL AND TYPE OF DEMAND EXPECTED*

Based on past experience, it appears that agencies will have a high demand for evaluation projects in the Individual Consumer Market. The evaluation offices of those agencies seem fully capable of generating enough demand to meet any likely budget.

We have argued that, in practice, serving the Individual Consumer Market usually means that there will be few restrictions placed on how the evaluation resources will be spent. The nature of the efforts undertaken will be determined by the type of consumer served and their interests.[2] Evaluation offices serving this market in ADAMHA have funded a broad range of efforts including:

- development of program reporting systems;
- development of an NIMH evaluation system;
- development of evaluation systems for grantees, including state and local communities;
- development of an evaluation system for regional offices;
- evaluation and monitoring of research and demonstration projects;
- measurement of the effectiveness of program treatment on clients;
- development of program standards;
- short-term analyses;
- analysis of decision making in a program area;

---

2. See Appendix C for a recent DHEW definition of evaluation which specifies a broad range of "eligible" evaluation activities.

- assessments of selected project activities (e.g., juvenile offender services); and
- assessments of ADAMHA's internal programs (e.g., scientific information services).

In contrast, another DHEW evaluation office serving one customer produces primarily short-term (six-month) analytical studies of interest to that customer.

The quality standards which studies must meet in this market are simply those demanded by each customer. There have been frequent complaints from both ASPE and ASH that many of the project proposals they receive from evaluation offices are of poor quality design or are inappropriate for evaluation funds. Many of these complaints may be well-founded. Yet they often ignore the fact that different user needs imply varying levels of quality; i.e., a particular customer need might be satisfied by a level of quality that would not satisfy "scientific standards." A single quality standard, even assuming one could be developed, might well be inappropriate because it would lead to more expensive studies than are required to satisfy individual needs. We do not argue for poor quality; rather, we believe that the quality of a study should be defined in the context of the intended use of the information. In the Individual Consumer Market, the consumer is in the best position to understand his need. (It may well be advisable for an evaluation office to explore that need with the consumer so that both agree on the quality required.) The Urban Institute experience with NIMH indicates, further, that there are also few incentives for an evaluation office to impose *stricter* standards on either the type or quality of studies than are required by the agency consumers. The standards suggested (but never documented) by higher levels (ASH and ASPE) are, as noted, frequently peripheral to individual consumer needs. Were it arbitrarily to impose these standards, an evaluation office might find its customers unable to comply, thus creating an artificial funding bottleneck,[3] rendering the evaluation office unable to meet the real demand.

3. *IMPLICATIONS FOR ORGANIZING AN EVALUATION OFFICE*

Serving the Individual Consumer Market imposes no strict organizational requirements on an evaluation office. Obviously a number of activities have to

---

3. See *Evaluation Planning at the National Institute of Mental Health: A Case History* by Pamela Horst, *et al.*, p. 158.

be carried out in producing evaluation studies, since they have to be selected, designed, executed, and disseminated. Responsibility for these activities can be held by the evaluation office or be delegated to another agency unit. The studies can be done in-house by the evaluation office or by outside contractors. In the latter case, RFPs would have to be prepared and the contractor would have to be monitored by either the evaluation office or the consumer.

The evaluation office has to carry out at least three core activities:

- operate the process through which evaluation projects are selected;
- meet DHEW evaluation planning requirements (e.g., DHEW usually requires an annual evaluation plan); and
- develop the evidence on evaluation office performance that it requires to manage its activities effectively and justify itself to external reviewers.

The first of these activities involves analysis of the customer's evaluation needs and interaction with the customer to reach agreement on the project required. As noted earlier, the evaluation office can do this very informally and with little time and effort, or quite intensively. An intensive effort could take up to two or three manmonths of evaluation staff time per customer. We view this activity as stopping short of the technical design of a study, and nontechnical staff might therefore be sufficient. The second core activity refers to the workload imposed on the evaluation office by the various DHEW evaluation planning and review requirements. These alone can take three to six manmonths of effort to complete. The final activity is the formal or informal survey of consumers to estimate evaluation office success. This type of work does not impose severe workload requirements—one or two manweeks per customer.

In addition to these core activities, there are others associated with evaluation project design, execution, and dissemination which may or may not be carried out by the evaluation office. In an agency, evaluation can be organized in such a way that different activities (beyond core activities) and different organizational models are required.

The range of possible organizational approaches can be characterized by four evaluation office activity models: *coordination, analytical, centralized administrative* and *decentralized administrative.*

The *coordination model* has the evaluation office carrying out only the three core activities. All other responsibilities are delegated to the customer. (This is an extreme form of the decentralized administrative model.)

The *analytical model* has the evaluation office staff doing the studies in-house in addition to performing the core activities. Staff members design the studies and execute them. Contractors, if hired, are used to carry out specific data collection or analysis tasks under the supervision of the evaluation staff. This model requires a highly technical staff.

The *administrative models* have the study designed and executed by a contracting process which, itself, requires a number of administrative tasks to be carried out. In the *centralized administrative model*, these tasks are the responsibility of the evaluation office; in the *decentralized administrative model*, they are shared by the customer and the evaluation office as illustrated in Table 3.

TABLE 3: PRIMARY RESPONSIBILITY FOR EVALUATION OFFICE ACTIVITIES IN AN ADMINISTRATIVE MODEL

Administrative Activity	Centralized	Decentralized
Develop RFPs	EO	EO, IC*
Select Contractors	EO	EO, IC
Monitor Contractors	EO	IC
Review Product	EO	IC, EO
Disseminate Product	EO	IC

*EO = Evaluation Office
 IC = Individual Consumer (e.g., program office staff)

The *centralized administrative model* does not require a technical staff. Usually one full-time staff member can handle the administrative responsibilities of a large number of studies (five to ten). The *decentralized model* has an evaluation office moving more toward a coordinating role. Since many of the administrative tasks are the responsibility of the customer, the *decentralized* evaluation office needs fewer staff people than the *centralized model* does.

Which model is most appropriate for serving this market? Any one will work and we have observed each in operation. The decision is usually predetermined by organizational factors such as the availability of personnel slots and the priority given to evaluation. It is difficult to say which model an organization should start with. Once one is in operation, its performance can be used as a guide to modifying the evaluation office design (see discussion in Chapter IV).

C. THE PROGRAM MANAGEMENT MARKET

1. *DEFINING THE INFORMATION NEEDED BY THE MARKET*

To serve the Program Management Market, an evaluation office must know:

- what programs are to be evaluated;
- who are the program managers;
- what is the program design and what evaluation information is feasible to develop; and
- what management use is there for the evaluation.[4]

The first two questions are best answered by the agency itself. An initial step in a comprehensive definition of programs is for the evaluation office, preferably through the agency director, to request each organization to provide a list of program titles that (a) are ranked by total annual budget (including federal staff budget), and (b) include all the activities within that organization (except for administration and staff offices). We also assume that such a list could be developed easily from document sources (the budget, a forward plan, internal planning documents). The listing is intended to provide a first cut at defining the units of analysis for evaluation planning purposes. It is important to remember that we are discussing *program* evaluation. Studies in this category will be focused on the performance of programs against defined objectives and tests of causal relationships.

Once programs and program management have been identified, the last two questions must be answered. Frequently, written documents and legislation are not suitable for establishing the program design because goals and objectives are not stated in measurable terms and do not adequately define actual management intentions. Here, then, the evaluation office must interact with program management to develop answers meaningful to management. The second year of our work with NIMH was directed to the development of a technique for answering these questions. The technique, called "evaluability assessment," was tested and found to be effective in (a) getting program management to specify their real program designs in measurable terms, (b) identifying potentially useful

---

4. A key question that arises in connection with management use is, how likely is it that any evaluation study could result in change to the program design? Older programs tend to have more "entrenched" designs and may prove to be much more difficult to affect. This argument, if true, may suggest that much stronger, more convincing evidence is required to change an older program than one relatively recently enacted.

evaluation studies, and (c) reaching agreement on whether management was interested in specific evaluation studies.

In brief, evaluability assessments[5] are reviews of program designs which are conducted by the evaluation office to help reach agreement with management on:

- measurable objectives;
- program activities linked to objectives; and
- testable hypotheses about the causal link between activities and objectives.

The product of the evaluability assessment is an "evaluable" program design—a program design which can be evaluated and which reflects management's intentions. Ideally a program evaluability assessment would result in one statement of the program design agreed to by all concerned managers. Practically, we believe that a different program design (certainly different objectives and measures) might well result for each organization level involved in the assessment (if one included, for example, ASPE, ASH, ADAMHA and NIMH). Should this occur, there are two options open to the evaluation office. It can attempt to reconcile divergent views by suggesting that all "managers" meet jointly until a single design statement is agreed upon. (The authors recognize that such a task is difficult, time consuming, and, in some cases, inconclusive.) Secondly, the evaluation office can simply accept the fact that different conceptions of the program exist and that different studies are necessary.

Once the evaluable program design is available, the evaluation office can identify potentially useful types of studies. It must then consult with management at different levels to determine which types appear useful to management. The overall result of the assessment can range from a number of potentially useful studies being done[6] to no useful studies being identified.

These steps are designed to limit evaluation studies to those that are feasible and useful. They imply more direct and intense participation in evaluation planning by line management than currently exists in most agencies. The purpose is to minimize subsequent line management attempts to "disown" evaluation studies with whose findings they disagree.

---

5. For a fuller explanation of evaluability assessment, refer to Appendix A.

6. Appendix B describes an alternative to an immediate full-scale evaluation called "rapid feedback evaluation." It is a preliminary study (internal or contracted) that collects and analyzes all existing information and results in (1) an assessment of what is already known and the quality of that information, and (2) evaluation design options for obtaining missing information.

2. *SERVING THE MARKET: THE LEVEL
AND TYPE OF DEMAND EXPECTED*

Our prior experience suggests that the demand for evaluation in the Program Management Market may be relatively low compared to the demand in the Individual Consumer Market.

During FY 1974, The Urban Institute and the NIMH Evaluation Branch carried out "evaluability assessments" on a number of NIMH programs.[7] We were attempting to identify studies which were needed by program managers and which were feasible, given the program as defined by management. Our principal findings were as follow:

- *Few program evaluations were feasible.* The programs as defined by program managers consisted, for the most part, of objectives for which measures had not been established and for which statements of testable hypotheses linking activities to objectives had not been defined. Thus the programs within NIMH lacked the necessary prerequisites for carrying out performance evaluation for most of their stated objectives. The evaluations which were feasible were relatively simple studies (e.g., compliance to guidelines, or the economic viability of projects after discontinuation of federal funds).

- *Program managers were unable to define how they would use evaluations and expressed little interest in the set of feasible studies.*[8]

- *Program managers were a significant part of the Individual Consumer Market.* Program managers frequently requested studies unrelated to the evaluation of their on-going programs. A primary interest of one program manager appeared to be the redesign of his program (setting objectives and specifying activities) and he saw the evaluation office as a source of contract support for such work. Other program managers requested evaluation funds to augment components of their program. Very little interest was expressed in "program evaluation"--assessment of the effectiveness of on-going program activities in achieving their objectives.

While these results apply to only one agency (and a narrow definition of management), it is our experience with other agencies and departments that the demand for studies in the Program Management Market is likely to be small. The type of studies that are feasible are likely to be methodologically straightforward and require little method development or technical sophistication.

---

7. See Pamela Horst, et al, *Evaluation Planning at the National Institute of Mental Health: A Case History*, The Urban Institute, 1974, Chapter V.

8. Program management was restricted to only one organizational level--the direct line manager (division or branch chief). Had we included agency management (NIMH director), there may have been more interest in those studies identified as feasible.

The important point for evaluation office planning is that the demand in any agency is uncertain until the evaluability assessments are carried out on its programs.

3. IMPLICATIONS FOR ORGANIZING AN EVALUATION OFFICE

In serving the Program Management Market, the evaluation office has to carry out three core activities:

- evaluability assessment of programs;[9]
- meet DHEW evaluation planning requirements (e.g., submission of annual plan); and
- develop the evidence on evaluation office performance that it requires to manage and justify itself.

The other activities necessary to produce and disseminate studies are not necessarily carried out by the evaluation office.

As with the Individual Consumer Market, we can distinguish four models of evaluation office organization with different staff requirements.

The *coordination model* has the evaluation office carrying out only the above three core activities (these activities are different in substance from the core activities of the other markets). All other responsibilities are delegated to program management. These core activities place higher workload requirements on the evaluation office than do the core activities of the Individual Consumer Market. Evaluability assessment is, in our experience, a time-consuming activity. It requires interaction with a number of organizational units to reach agreement on program design. Frequently program designs are in a state of change or debate and coming to some agreement may take time. We estimate that the evaluability assessment takes on the order or two to three manmonths per program. The other two core activities would require totally at least one full-time person. Thus, for an agency with a dozen programs singled out for evaluation, the Program Management Market would require a full-time staff of approximately four people.

The other three possible models--analytical, centralized administrative and decentralized administrative--are the same as described under the Individual Consumer Market.

---

9. The technique described earlier and in Appendix A is one possible approach to conducting an evaluability assessment. The authors recognize that other techniques may be used to produce the same result.

Which of the four models is most appropriate for serving the Program Management Market? Our view is that either of the decentralized models would be most appropriate (at the present time); i.e., *coordination* or *decentralized administrative*. This judgment is based on two observations. First, we are uncertain as to the level of the demand for evaluation by program management. Our limited experience in measuring this demand suggests that few studies may be required. Second, our experience also indicates that those studies which are both feasible and useful will most likely be methodologically simple and straightforward. A strong central in-house technical capability may not be required in order to design studies or to monitor contractors. Until the evaluability assessments are done--and they take time--the evaluation office will not know its total workload (i.e., staff and funds required) or the type of studies actually required. Therefore, it might be more efficient to use a small evaluation staff to carry out the core functions and augment it on an *ad hoc* basis as individual studies are identified. The augmentation can be effected by having the program office (1) take responsibility for the study, (2) establish an independent task force to do the study or (3) reassign staff on a temporary basis to the evaluation office. However, we should note that we believe the other organizational models are *capable* of serving the Program Management Market.

D. THE POLICY MARKET

1. *DEFINING THE INFORMATION NEEDED BY THE MARKET*

    To serve the Policy Market, the evaluation office has to decide:
    - which policy debates it will address;
    - who the customer is (policy makers and those influencing opinion in the debate); and
    - what studies have potential for affecting opinions, attitudes, and positions.

For the Policy Market, even more than for the Program Management Market, the evaluation office must consider as its customers groups far removed from the agency. No one person and no limited number of people speak for the Policy Market.

The evaluation office will have to make judgmental decisions in answering the three questions. For this, three major sources of information are available to guide the evaluation office: the formal management processes which support decision making, the policy makers themselves, and the experience of the evaluation office staff.[10] Based on our review of selected DHEW management processes, we find that the formal documents in these processes provide important but limited guidance for planning a policy-oriented evaluation study. The reason for this limitation is that they rarely contain any information about the basis used to make decisions or even to propose particular programs or policies. One has the impression that the formal documents (particularly in forward planning and budgeting) represent a kind of shorthand to the major participants, a set of key words that remind everyone of what it is they are debating. Further, a number of interviewees indicated that many of the proposals and the arguments had been heard before--indeed we were told that truly new proposals are seldom, if ever, floated for the first time in the forward plan. Instead, new proposals are debated and cleared through bureaucratic channels months in advance of the formal planning process.

In reviewing the formal budgeting process, it is easy to place mistaken emphasis on any one particular document. However, if one only tracks the various budget submissions and changes through the system, one misses the real decision process almost completely. Despite the many changes that occur and appear in one submission or another, the formal documents capture only a relatively small part of the decisions and revisions that *are* the budget process, but are not reflected on paper. Our assessment of budgeting indicates that the budget process tracks decisions as they are made, but that the documents rarely indicate why they are made or who the principle decision makers are. Nevertheless, through its reviews of the formal outputs of management processes (forward plan, budget), the evaluation office should be able to define a set of issues and gain some information on the organizational units participating in the debates. The gathering of this information is one of the steps

---

10. The government decision process, which affects DHEW, can only be characterized at a very high level of abstraction. First, there are formal components--those parts which are governed by procedures and schedules such as the budget process. Included here are the DHEW management systems designed to support decision making, such as OPS and forward planning. There is also the complex informal decision process in which members of the Policy Market debate, communicate, compromise, and decide. It is informal in that it is not governed by procedures, formats, or schedules.

the evaluation office should perform in evaluation planning. With respect to the other information sources specified above, there are two options open to an evaluation office attempting to serve the Policy Market. One is to rely upon its own experience and judgment to determine the most important issues under debate, the beliefs held by the participants in the debate, and the decision basis those participants are using at the moment. The second option is to conduct a survey of policy makers, formally and informally, to define the same information. Because evaluation offices are normally part of a large planning *and* evaluation office, the survey approach may be an unnecessary cost that adds only marginally to the information readily available within the larger office. Evaluation offices will need to use their own judgment to determine for each issue whether the survey cost (in terms of their own time) is acceptable given their perceived need to define such information or verify what information they already have.

We summarize below the planning steps that an evaluation office would need to complete (with the understanding that survey interviews might not be necessary):

- Review formal policy-making processes to identify key issues and interfaces. Rank the issues in order of importance to the agency and develop a list of participants in the decision process to be interviewed (agency management might take a strong role in ranking the issues).

- Carry out interviews (or rely upon evaluation office experience) to determine the opinions and positions of the participants on the issue and the basis on which the issue is expected to be resolved. We stress here again that serving this market requires exploration of the needs of many, if not all, of the participants. The complex nature of policy making, in which so many are involved, precludes the possibility of impacting the market by serving only one or two participants. (Indeed in serving only one participant the evaluation office reverts to serving the Individual Consumer Market.)

- With the results of the survey (however informal), the evaluation office will have to make assumptions about which types of studies would be likely to influence the opinion and positions of participants. It can be expected that statements of issues will not directly imply or suggest specific studies and study designs.

- The evaluation office must ultimately decide which studies would be most likely to influence the opinions of the group involved in the debate. At this point, the evaluation office might ask outside experts or panels of participants in the debate to review the technical soundness and policy relevance of its study design.

- The final step in the planning process should be the development of a dissemination strategy for each study which will permit the evaluation office to measure its impact as discussed in Chapter IV.

2. *SERVING THE MARKET: THE LEVEL AND TYPE OF DEMAND EXPECTED*

It is difficult to speculate on how much of a demand there is for evaluation information in the Policy Market. Given a fixed budget and a technically competent staff, experience indicates that an evaluation office can select and design sufficient evaluation studies to consume that budget.[11] The real question is, however, how many studies have the potential for influencing the Policy Market? Since no one has ever attempted to answer the question systematically, there is no experience to go by. An evaluation office serving this market will be attempting to *create a demand* while at the same time running an experiment to see if the demand is realized.

There are two major conflicting theories about the type of information which will impact on the Policy Market. One argument holds that evaluation studies must produce high-quality information with high levels of confidence, because a large number of diverse individuals and groups must be influenced. This assumption translates into large-scale data collection efforts with sophisticated research designs to account for various effects. (The term often used is "quasi-experimental designs.") Critics counter that planning and execution of such studies takes two to three years while policy issues are usually raised and resolved within one-half to one year. Moreover, the whole character and make-up of the policy arena can change within one year. Therefore, they call for short-term studies on the order of six months which stress analysis of existing data and synthesis of existing knowledge (although new data collection is not ruled out).

Which type of information is most effective is an open question. The evaluation office would have to make a decision on a case-by-case basis and use feedback on evaluation office performance to judge its own decisions.

---

11. See *Federal Evaluation Policy* by Joseph S. Wholey, John W. Scanlon, Hugh G. Duffy, James S. Fukumoto, and Leona M Vogt, Washington, D. C., The Urban Institute, 1970, for a discussion of OEO's central evaluation office.

3. *IMPLICATIONS FOR ORGANIZING AN EVALUATION OFFICE*

To serve the Policy Market, the evaluation office has to carry out three core activities:

- Carry out a survey and analysis of the Policy Market to identify studies with potential for impact.
- Meet DHEW evaluation planning requirements.
- Develop the evidence on evaluation office performance that it requires to manage and justify its activities.

These core activities are very different from those suggested for the other two markets. They require a more technical and analytical staff and a workload comparable to that imposed by the evaluability assessments in the Program Management Market. We estimate that the survey and analysis of the Policy Market would require two to three manmonths of effort per issue. If the evaluation office decides that it needs formal surveys to produce acceptable levels of evidence, an additional two to three months of effort would be required per study. Both activities would require technical staff.

Four models of evaluation office organization were identified earlier: coordination, analytical, decentralized administrative and centralized administrative. The models chosen here imply the capability to design and produce either high-quality quick analyses or quasi-experiments, as discussed above. For serving the Policy Market, the two decentralized models—*coordination* and *decentralized administrative*—would, therefore, appear to be inappropriate for most agencies simply because there is no obvious group with technical expertise to whom responsibility could be delegated. The *analytical* and *centralized administrative* models (or some combination of the two) seem more appropriate. The size of the staff requirement in either model would depend on the type of studies done. If we assume that the *analytical* model would be best suited for doing short-term studies in-house, then we would estimate two full-time staff members could turn out one study in six months. If we assume that the centralized administrative model is better suited for the large-scale field studies, then we estimate that one full-time staff member with a technical background could monitor one or two large studies at the same time. (A large study would be on the order of $.5 million to $1 million.)

E. COMPARISON OF THE REQUIREMENTS IMPOSED BY THE MARKETS

The evaluation markets do not call for any single type of study. It is possible (but unlikely) that three evaluation offices, each serving a different market, might do the same studies. And conversely, given a market, the type of study called for will still vary from customer to customer.

The markets do impose certain activities on the evaluation office. We have defined these requirements as the *core activities* of the evaluation office—activities that an evaluation office has to carry out to serve a particular market.

Table 4 identifies the core activities and provides gross estimates of the staff requirements necessary to carry them out. (These estimates would have to be adjusted for any given agency to reflect agency size, programs, etc.) The activities imposed by the market in planning studies and developing evidence on study impact differ from market to market as reflected in the different staffing requirements.

In addition to the core activities, other activities have to be carried out to design, produce, and disseminate studies. To reflect the fact that these activities can be carried out by the evaluation office, or a contractor, or some other unit in the agency, models of four types of evaluation offices were identified:

- *coordination model*—the evaluation office staff carries out only the core activities;
- *analytical model*—the evaluation office staff designs and executes studies in-house;
- *administrative, centralized*—study design and execution contracted out, evaluation staff maintains administrative responsibility for the contract; and
- *administrative, decentralized*—study design and execution contracted out, evaluation staff shares administrative responsibility with other agency units.

The market does not impose strict requirements for one model over another. However, in our judgment, certain models are usually more appropriate for serving certain markets. Our views are summarized in Table 5. All four models are shown being equally suitable for serving the Individual Consumer Market. The "best" one for a particular agency depends on the types of evaluation projects requested and the availability of in-house staff resources.

TABLE 4: ESTIMATED STAFF REQUIREMENTS FOR THE CORE EVALUATION OFFICE ACTIVITIES*

Federal Evaluation Market	Core Activities	Estimated Staff Requirements
Individual Consumer Market	(1) Operate the study selection process. (2) Meet DHEW planning requirements. (3) Develop evidence on evaluation office performance.	• Negotiation with consumer and analyses of need: level of effort can vary; 2-3 manmonths per customer could be required; staff with administrative background. • Activities (2) and (3): one full-time staff, administrative background.
Program Management Market	(1) Evaluability assessment of programs. (2) Meet DHEW planning requirements. (3) Develop evidence on evaluation office performance.	• Evaluability assessments: 2-3 manmonths per program, some technical background. • Activities (2) and (3): one full-time staff, administrative background.
Policy Market	(1) Survey and analyze Policy Market. (2) Meet DHEW planning requirements. (3) Develop evidence on evaluation office performance.	• Survey and analysis of market: 2-3 manmonths per issue; strong technical background. • DHEW planning requirements: 1-2 manmonths, administrative background. • Develop evidence: 2-3 manmonths per study (formal surveys); some technical background.

*See Table 6 where we identify the other activities an evaluation office would have to carry out in addition to the core activities.

TABLE 5: PREFERRED ORGANIZATIONAL MODELS FOR
SERVING FEDERAL EVALUATION MARKETS

Organizational Models	Individual Consumer	Program Management	Policy
Coordination	+	+	-
Analytical	+	0	+
Administrative, Centralized	+	0	+
Administrative, Decentralized	+	+	-

Symbols: + = model is one preferred for serving the market
0 = model is acceptable but not preferred
- = model is inappropriate

TABLE 6: ADDITIONAL STAFF REQUIREMENTS FOR
THE ORGANIZATIONAL MODELS*

Organizational Model	Estimated Additional Staff Requirements
Coordination	None.
Analytical	In-house, technical staff. Difficult to estimate workload since type of study required can vary. One estimate: 2 full-time staff members producing, on the average, one study in six months.
Administrative, Centralized	For high-quality, large-scale contract studies: 1 full-time, technical person per one or two studies.
	For studies with fewer agency requirements: 1 full-time, nontechnical person per five to ten studies.
Administrative, Decentralized	One or two full-time, nontechnical staff with administrative responsibilities.

*All models carry out the core activities with the staffing requirements given in Table 4. These requirements are *in addition* to those of the core activities.

The Program Management Market can also be served by all four models; however, two are preferred--the coordination and the administrative decentralized. The other two provide more resources than the demand may warrant based on our present knowledge. The Policy Market is capable of being served by the analytical and administrative, centralized models. The other two do not provide the staff resources necessary to plan and execute the required studies.

An evaluation office should carry out the core activities. In addition to the staff necessary for core activities, the organizational model chosen may have other staff requirements. It is difficult to estimate total staff requirements for these models because they can be used to produce all types of studies. Table 6 provides some tentative guidance on the type of workload estimates that might be required for various models.

We have observed all four types of organizational models in DHEW. Tables 4-6 suggest that an evaluation office, as it currently operates, may be locked in to serving only one market. It may not have the necessary staff or skills to serve a certain market. This is one of the constraints that an evaluation office manager must consider and deal with. How an evaluation office can address this problem is discussed in Chapter VI.

VI. APPLICATION OF THE MARKET APPROACH

A. INTRODUCTION

As we observed earlier, two problems confront DHEW evaluation today. First, while evaluation offices often define objectives, they fail to specify adequate measures of success. Second, there is no concensus among federal actors concerning what particular objectives or success criteria evaluation offices should adopt. In short, there is no federal evaluation policy. The symptoms of these problems are easily discerned. Lacking success criteria, evaluation offices are often uncertain how to plan and organize their efforts. Further compounding the difficulty, evaluation offices undergo frequent criticism from a variety of actors, each using *different* assumptions about the nature of evaluation, the group it should serve, and the effects it should bring about.

The Urban Institute has developed a market approach designed to address these two problems. The approach has the following elements and characteristics:

- We define three markets in terms of organizational units which are performing a function or activity. The market definitions are operational, not prescriptive, in the sense that we describe the procedures the evaluation office itself can use to define the market.

- We define evaluation office objectives in terms of how the office intends to affect each market, and provide measures for determining whether the desired effects have been achieved. Success measures are accompanied by different methods of collecting evidence of performance.

- Finally, we define a different set of minimum requirements for serving each market. Requirements govern study characteristics, staffing, resources, and staff activity.

We believe the market approach can affect the problems described above by (1) assisting evaluation offices to plan their programs, (2) clarifying debate between evaluation offices and reviewers (ASH, ASPE, OMB, GAO, etc.) and (3) providing an orderly basis for debating the parameters of a federal evaluation policy. Each of these uses of the approach will be described briefly below. Of course, were a workable federal evaluation policy extant, the need to use such an approach in the first two instances would be substantially minimized. Therefore, use of the market approach to plan evaluation and clarify review debates is described in the present-day context, where little agreement exists on the purpose and desired effects of evaluation.

B. USING THE MARKET APPROACH TO GUIDE EVALUATION OFFICE PLANNING

The evaluation office must determine at some point what market it will serve as well as what success criteria to use. In particular, evaluation offices must consider the discretion they have to set their own objectives in the agency and the need to respond to outside reviewers.

Our observations lead us to believe that evaluation offices may not be entirely free to serve any market they choose. At present, most DHEW federal-level evaluation offices serve the Individual Consumer Market exclusively. It may be argued that this condition exists because it is easiest to serve the Individual Consumer Market—the activities involved require a lower degree of technical skill and a smaller staff. Therefore, certain evaluation groups may have chosen this market as the line of least resistance. On the other hand, we believe that internal political forces in the agency are the most potent factor in diverting evaluation offices to serve the Individual Consumer Market rather than policy and program decision makers. For example, a top agency official may require that the evaluation office produce short-term evaluation studies tailored to meet the needs of his office. Under these circumstances, the evaluation office has little negotiating room to move out of the Individual Consumer Market. Another restricting factor is the high level of demand placed on "1 percent" funds by individual consumers who have few alternative sources of support for research, analytical studies, data collection, etc. Were a shift to a different market to squeeze or cut off available 1 percent funds, individual consumers might attempt to work around or undermine the evaluation office policy. This phenomenon partly explains the decision of NIMH to terminate its draft evaluation policy designed to serve the Program Management Market. Consumer complaints over disapproved studies, coupled with disagreement in the OPPE over the new market objectives, also caused a shift back into serving the Individual Consumer Market.

The ability of the evaluation office to move into the Policy and Program Management Markets is heavily contingent upon the existing or potential degree of organizational support. There are several possible situations. (1) If the evaluation office does have organizational support, it should nevertheless move slowly for two reasons. First, it is essential to test the market demand, particularly for policy studies, because the level of demand has not been established with any certainty. Second, a modest first-year investment in no more than one or two studies is suggested to allow evaluation planners the time to test and refine new techniques. In particular, the evaluability assessments or policy surveys should be reviewed to assure they were conducted in the most useful manner. (2) On the other hand, if the evaluation office has no support for a market shift, it can still attempt to move slowly into a new market, trying to build support through a series of negotiations as planning proceeds. In this situation, evaluation offices may find it easier to develop support for program management rather than policy studies, as the former are more directly connected with the agency's self-interests.[1] (3) If there is active antagonism within the agency to serving new markets, the evaluation office will not have the option to proceed with new market development. It can continue to serve the Individual Consumer Market where the demand had proven substantial. If the evaluation office deems it necessary, it can work to develop or improve the evidence which measures consumer satisfaction with its products.

ADAMHA appears to fit the third case. There is no evidence to suggest that resistance encountered in 1973 to serving only the Program Management Market has diminished since that time. Further restricting ADAMHA's current discretion are staff limitations and unclear authority *vis-à-vis* the institutes. ADAMHA has one half-time staff member assigned to evaluation, and the institute evaluation offices each have no more than one full-time equivalent, a complement of staff inadequate to carry out the activities required to serve the Program Management and Policy Markets. Thus, ADAMHA appears to have little discretionary authority in developing new market activity.

The evaluation office itself must assess the degree of threat posed by critical reviews. Some offices may decide to ignore criticism and not develop performance objectives and success evidence in the belief that there is no

---
1. It has been pointed out by agency evaluators, however, that program managers also have more to lose through evaluation.

systematic accountability--that the office will not be penalized or forced to change as a result of critical outside reviews. The threat of critical review may prompt others to replan. While we know of no instances where adverse reviews of evaluation office operations resulted in loss of funding or personnel slots, nonetheless, adverse criticism can diminish the status of the evaluation office in the eyes of its host or other agencies, thereby reducing its influence. Accumulated critical reviews have also provoked reorganizations, particularly the formation of centralized evaluation offices which assume some control functions normally carried out at lower levels. (ASPE's dominant role in evaluation, for example, was formed under these circumstances.)

C. USING THE MARKET APPROACH TO CLARIFY DEBATES BETWEEN THE EVALUATION OFFICE AND REVIEW GROUPS

Evaluation office operations and performance are periodically reviewed by groups from the Office of the Secretary, GAO and OMB. These efforts are frequently nonproductive, and occasionally counterproductive, for two reasons:

- Reviewers lack a basis for sorting through the mass of evaluation studies and planning statements to arrive at a fair and accurate appraisal.
- Evaluation offices view the critiques, which are usually negative, as highly judgmental, of questionable validity, and as offering little constructive guidance.

The net result is that the reviewer and reviewee talk past one another.

If we assume that these nonroutine reviews will occur in an environment where there is no agreed-upon federal evaluation policy, how can the review process be made more productive? We believe that both parties can better participate in reviews by using the evaluation market approach to design their review procedures.

Reviewers should begin an assessment of agency evaluation with an analysis of the evaluation office's (1) objectives and success criteria and (2) the organizational conditions which determined (set) those objectives. A systematic procedure, similar to "evaluability assessments" for programs, should be conducted by the reviewer in which he:

- extracts from evaluation office documentation and staff interviews the objectives, success criteria, and level of evidence developed by the office;
- separates objectives into those which are rhetorical and those which are evaluable; and

- verifies that the real evaluation office objectives and evidence have been identified by discussing the results with the evaluation office.

Using this approach, the reviewer can shortcut most of the traditional review activity by simply questioning the evaluation office chief in two areas: How are you measuring evaluation office success? Why type of evidence do you collect? Examination of the measures and evidence will allow the reviewer to distinguish which markets are being served. If the evaluation office does not collect evidence on an objective, then, by definition, it is not "managing" its activities to meet that objective. Thus, the reviewer is afforded a rapid way of determining what the office is attempting to accomplish. He saves time, avoids rhetorical traps, and avoids fruitless debate where both parties argue from different premises concerning the actual mission of the evaluation office. Once the evaluable objectives are identified, the reviewer can:

- raise issues about whether or not these objectives are the right ones;
- raise issues about whether the level of evidence collected is adequate for management and justification; and
- assess whether or not the evaluation office is adequately meeting its evaluable objectives.

As discussed earlier, the first two issues may be beyond the authority of the evaluation office. Once the reviewer examines the organizational conditions which determined those objectives, he may find it necessary to go to other organizational units to argue for a change.

Since the evaluation office is a participant in the review, it can prepare itself for such occasions. If evaluation offices model their operations on the market approach, they are in a better position to explain their mission and justify their activities. They can also identify and fend off criticism which stems from an erroneous view of evaluation office objectives. For example, a reviewer might find the quality of studies produced for the Individual Consumer Market to be deficient. In response, the evaluation office may clearly point out that its objective is not the production of studies to meet some arbitrary scientific standard but, rather, the production of studies which satisfy the perceived needs of individual consumers. Further, a clear, concise explanation of evaluation office objectives, success criteria, and evidence may disarm reviewers who do not have well-articulated counter proposals.

We do not mean to imply that use of the approach will silence debate altogether. Inevitably, reviewers will question the appropriateness of actual evaluation office objectives, criteria for success, and the breakpoint at which successful performance is revealed. However, the use of the market approach will help to minimize counterproductive debate based on different assumptions about what the evaluation office is trying to accomplish.

D. USING THE MARKET APPROACH TO ESTABLISH A FEDERAL EVALUATION POLICY

The term *federal evaluation policy* refers to policies which might be established governmentwide or by a single department. This report has stated that there is no *federal evaluation policy*. We mean that, in practice, every agency is free to do what it wishes in evaluation--department guidances do not guide, outside reviews have little effect. Most importantly, there is no established procedure for reaching agreement on evaluation office objectives, success criteria, and required levels of evidence.

Many have felt a need to establish evaluation policies for the government, a department, or a program. The question arises, why develop a federal evaluation policy at all? The efforts in this direction have occurred primarily because the evaluation information produced has not been viewed as useful to two particular markets: Program Management and Policy. In particular, GAO, OMB, and the Office of the Secretary have expressed dissatisfaction with the performance of evaluation in serving the Policy and Program Management Markets. They feel that program managers and policy makers lack sufficient evaluative information to do their jobs well. These groups have been equally critical of the studies produced for the Individual Consumer Market, citing poor study methodology, inadequate analysis, and low utilization. As we pointed out earlier, however, current organizational incentives and staffing limitations seem to encourage service to individual consumers and to inhibit significant movement into the Program Management and Policy Markets. In principal, a formal federal evaluation policy would provide GAO, OMB, and OS with the vehicle for establishing the incentives[2] and protections necessary for evaluation

---

2. It has been observed that incentives without adequate staff might still confront small evaluation offices with only one option--continue to operate as they presently do.

offices to begin serving new markets, while at the same time legitimizing work performed to satisfy individual consumers.

It is by no means clear cut that the criticisms leveled by GAO, OMB, etc., are valid or that the information gaps they perceive are real. It is not clear because *no one has demonstrated that any substantial level of demand for studies exists in either the Program Management Market or the Policy Market.* A systematic examination of this issue may show that serving the Individual Consumer Market is *the* best way and *the* only way for an evaluation office to serve government. Given this uncertainty in market demand, we feel that evaluation policy makers should move cautiously in establishing a federal evaluation policy. We recommend that:

- any policy that is adopted be designed and implemented using the market approach--specification of market objectives, measurable success criteria, and type of acceptable evidence; and

- any evaluation policy directed at serving markets other than the individual consumer be based on a series of careful experiments set up to measure demand.

What should be the characteristics of a federal evaluation policy? It may contain guidance on organization and staffing, *although we believe that several organizational models can serve a single market equally well.* It may prescribe certain planning and administrative activities, or define levels of review and control over studies proposed for funding. *We believe, however, that if it does nothing else, a federal evaluation policy must define market objectives, specify measurable success criteria and specify the types of evidence acceptable for demonstrating performance.* Further, those objectives and success criteria must be negotiated with each level to be held accountable. From the policy failures described in Chapter II, it is evident that certain design features should be avoided. Evaluation policies characterized by unmeasurable definitional sets (classes of data, types of decisions, types of evaluations to be produced, etc.) have exerted no discernible effect on evaluation office activity, only on the rhetoric included in plans. Policies attempting to influence the character of the study solely through adjustments in the nature and sequence of planning steps have proven equally unsuccessful.

How can evaluation policy makers (ASH, ASPE, OMB) move efficiently to develop a realistic policy? We recommend a three-step process:

- conduct a survey of evaluation offices to determine the market served;

- test the level of demand in the Policy and Program Management Markets; and
- use the market approach as a vehicle for debating the parameters of a federal evaluation policy.

First, we recommend a survey of evaluation offices to determine the markets presently served. The survey would examine the nature of the success measures employed, the evidence collected to assess performance and the pressures dictating market choices. To save time and effort, it may be desirable to survey offices on a sample, not an inclusive basis, if this can be done without unreasonable deterioration in validity and reliability. Survey findings could be used to define with some certainty what markets are currently being served, why those markets were selected, and the nature of the incentives needed to allow movement into the Policy and Program Management Markets.

Next, we believe it is necessary to test the level of demand in the Policy and Program Management Markets. In Chapters IV and V, we defined the objectives, success criteria, and core activities required to serve each market. What is needed is some testing, hopefully of a systematic nature, so that it can be learned whether evaluation products are needed in policy making and program management and whether these particular activities do produce the intended results. It is not necessary to test all activities simultaneously. For example, policy surveys can be conducted independently from evaluability assessments. Further, one sector, an agency for example, can be selected to test part or all of a new approach. The key to the validity of any test, however, is that it be assessed experimentally--with the intent to learn whether altered sets of activities produce the desired effects. Controls and information feedback will be necessary to assess the validity of hypotheses connecting activities with effects on policy or program management.

Finally, we suggest that the market approach be used to ground or organize a formal, federal-level debate whose outcome is the creation of a federal evaluation policy. At a minimum, the following questions must be addressed and resolved:

- What groups, performing what function, should be served by federal evaluation?
- What is the level of demand within each market?
- What constitutes desirable objectives for service to each market?
- What criteria and evidence are required to show successful service?
- How can the evaluation office define the information needs of each market?

- To serve each market successfully, what are the requirements for staff size, capability, and level of resources?
- How do these requirements compare with current resources?
- Should evaluation offices at different levels (e.g., institutes, ADAMHA, ASH, OS, etc.) serve different markets?

We believe the three steps suggested above (surveying evaluation office objectives, testing new market demand and activity, and using the market approach to organize formal federal debate) will contribute to the development of a federal evaluation policy. However, ADAMHA does not have the staff or resources to undertake these tasks. Therefore, we recommend that ADAMHA use its influence with ASH, ASPE, OMB, GAO, and others to press for negotiated agreement on evaluation office objectives, criteria for success, and appropriate levels of evidence. Such agreement would constitute the core requirement of a federal evaluation policy.

APPENDIX A

Assessment of Evaluability

ASSESSMENT OF EVALUABILITY

A. WHAT IS ASSESSMENT OF EVALUABILITY?

Program evaluation compares the program, as defined by management, with reality: the activities and effects actually occurring. An assessment of evaluability is an analytical process carried out prior to evaluation. It is conducted to define a program in terms that agree with a manager's intentions--what he thinks he is doing and is controlling--and with the evaluator's tasks--measurement, analysis, and feedback. The product of the evaluability assessment is a formal definition of the program and identification of the feasible evaluation studies that can be conducted. It represents the evaluator's first statement of what he can do for a manager.

B. WHY DO AN EVALUABILITY ASSESSMENT?

There are two reasons for conducting such an assessment: (1) to clarify and bound the evaluator's job; and (2) to clarify the manager's job.

1. *EVALUATION PLANNING*

Evaluators throughout the federal government are given budgets to evaluate the performance of federal programs. They are confronted with many options on ways to approach the evaluation function and, in most large organizations, with an insatiable desire for information. The evaluators are also confronted with a plaguing problem--utilization of their studies. There seems unanimous agreement on how to improve utilization, or even on whether or not the evaluator need worry about it. One of the major causes of the low use of evaluation studies is that most federal social programs are not sufficiently well-defined to lead to agreement among the management as to success criteria. The lack of agreement is manifested in the form of criticism, after the fact, with the findings of evaluation studies. Assessment of evaluability before the initiation of a study is a method of screening programs to determine in which programs and in which parts of programs there exists sufficient definition to make to make evaluation potentially useful. Evaluability assessments are most useful to evaluators seeking close links with program management and least useful to those evaluators who view their function as independent research.

2. *PROGRAM PLANNING*

Agency managers make decisions about their programs with or without information. They justify and allocate budgets; allocate staff to activities; recommend and implement changes to legislation, guidelines, and regulations; form task forces; and numerous other related activities. Many of the potential decisions are constrained by legislation, policy, or political considerations. Yet the managers also have discretion regarding internal staff activities, grants and contracts, and what changes they will attempt to introduce by influencing policy makers at a higher level.

One of the major difficulties facing a program manager is deciding what it is he is trying to accomplish. The failure to focus, to concentrate on achievable even if limited objectives, may well inhibit any accomplishment. The assessment of evaluability could, for the manager, be termed assessment of manageability--a definition of what it is he is managing.

C. HOW IS A PROGRAM ASSESSED?

Conducting an evaluability assessment involves a sequential series of steps which bound and refine the program from two perspectives, that of the manager and that of the evaluator. Each has something of value to bring to the assessment. The steps are:

- *Bounding the program:* Determining what federal, state, or local activities and what objectives constitute the program--what is the unit that is to be analyzed?

- *Collection of program information:* Gathering information that defines the program's objectives, activities, and underlying assumptions.

- *Modeling:* Development of a model that describes the program and the interrelationships of activities and objectives.

- *Analysis:* Determining to what extent the program definition, as represented by the model, is sufficiently unambiguous that evaluation is feasible and potentially useful. This step also includes the definition of potential evaluation studies.

- *Presentation to management:* Feedback of the results of the assessment to the program manager(s) and determination of next steps that should be taken.

1. *BOUNDING THE PROGRAM*

The first task is to decide what constitutes a federal program in order to define the unit to be analyzed. Virtually all federal agencies have a number of activities that are directly related to the legislative program (such as grant administration) and a number of activities that are supportive (research, evaluation, information systems, technical assistance). The question to consider is the following: Are all of these activities one program, or is each activity an independent program? (Many of these activities may be analagous to overhead in a commercial venture.) There is no formula for deciding what is a program and what is part of a program. Essentially we would attempt to determine which of the activities within a manager's purview are justified because of the existence of the legislative program and which have an independent life of their own. Research is often a difficult activity in which to determine relationships to programs. Does the research have its own objectives, broader than the program under analysis? Is it a necessary component of the program? Many programs begin with a research component focused on obtaining information for improvement of the program; subsequently, the research becomes extended to broader questions beyond the scope of the program. Whether research is part of a program or is independent, it is probably preferable, initially, to include activities rather than to exclude them.

The bounding exercise should also include an examination of which management levels are to be included in defining the program. When program objectives are to be examined, it is logical to ask whose objectives they are. Legislation is infrequently definitive on this point and many programs become tailored to meet the objectives of more than one manager. Within the federal bureaucracy, the branch, division, and at least one higher level should nominally be included.

2. *COLLECTION OF PROGRAM INFORMATION*

Having decided roughly the boundaries of the program to be assessed, it is necessary to collect information defining the program. Logical sources of information would include legislation, forward plans, budget justifications, internal division or branch plans, and interviews with program and agency management. The information to be collected would be objectives, activity descriptions, and any statements describing the activity-objective relationships. In most programs, there will be a set of objectives related in some hierarchical order or on some time-phased basis. The evaluator should try to get objective statements defined as precisely as possible in terms that are measurable. In getting this information, the evaluator is trying to develop a sense of how well the program manager has defined his own objectives. He is not attempting to question objectives at this stage, however. If a manager defines an objective and has no idea how it might be measured, that fact should be noted for future analysis.

During this part of the analysis, the evaluator must obtain enough time from agency and program managers to assure himself that he has a comprehensive description and understands the relationships of the component parts of the program. Reliance strictly on documentation (legislation, plans, etc.) will limit the ability of the evaluator to understand the manager's concept of his program.

3. *DEVELOPING THE RHETORICAL MODEL*

The next stage of analysis is to develop a model that captures the important intended relationships among activities and objectives. Methods other than modeling can and have been used to perform this function, but flow models appear to be a satisfactory and informative method for communicating quickly and effectively the component parts and relationships of federal program activities and objectives.

An important characteristic of the rhetorical program model is that it captures all of the activities and their objectives, while avoiding the temptation to insert what might appear to be missing or "necessary" objectives or activities. The rhetorical model should represent the program that has been defined by the manager and discussed in legislation, along with internal plans and program justifications. There is no rigid predefined model format used to convey this description of the program.

4. *ANALYSIS OF THE RHETORICAL MODEL*

From the evaluator's perspective, two tests need to be applied to the rhetorical model: (1) are the objectives stated in measurable terms; and (2) are there statements of hypotheses that are testable?

Measurability implies that agreement exists on the part of management as to what would constitute or signal success. Acceptable measures may be objective or subjective. There are really two parts to the question of measurability: (1) the indicator of achievement and (2) the means of verification. It is a standard part of program evaluation methodology that both indicators and means of verification be developed as part of any evaluation. The key question is, who should develop the measures of success? The assessment process discussed here rests on the belief that ambiguous objectives should not be rendered unambiguous by an evaluator; that, we believe, is a management prerogative. The analysis of objectives for measurability is not, then, a test of the evaluator's ingenuity in defining measures. It is, rather, a test to determine whether the manager has defined what he wants his program to accomplish and what evidence he needs to determine this. Lacking such measures, the objective is eliminated from the model, classified temporarily as "unmeasurable" (meaning only that no agreement exists at the moment on what evidence would signal success). The examination should include all objectives, not just the program "impact" objectives. This would certainly include the "process" objectives associated with staff research, technical assistance, or other administrative activities.

The second part of the assessment concerns the hypotheses linking activities to process objectives and process to program objectives. Ideally, the hypotheses would be explanations of causality that could be isolated through appropriate tests to provide feedback to a manager indicating that an observed effect was attributable to a particular set of activities and to no other variables. Practically, however, we must settle for substantially less in virtually all federal programs. The means of verification mentioned earlier is the test that a manager would consider adequate and feasible to demonstrate that his objective had been achieved and that the effect was at least plausibly related to his activities.

Taken together, the manager's definition of measurable objectives and testable hypotheses constitute his best statement of the evidence he needs to determine that his program is or is not proving to be effective. It is important to note that we are seeking the manager's definition, not the evaluator's. When more than one level of management is involved, it is likely that more than one set of definitions will emerge. In many cases, no acceptable definition will emerge. When there is no definition (managers do not know and cannot construct any adequate tests of their hypotheses), the hypotheses (links on the model between activities and objectives) are eliminated from the rhetorical model.

After eliminating from the model any objectives that are not currently measurable and any linking assumptions that have not yet been defined, a second "evaluable" program model is developed reflecting the remaining measurable activities, objectives, and testable assumptions. This evaluable model should reflect the manager's intention for the program. It is likely that the model will indicate many activities which are not linked to program objectives.

The evaluator then has an adequate basis to examine the program's potential and the manager's need for evaluation. From the evaluator's perspective, the evaluable program model represents a device to focus his information program, screening out not only the unanswerable questions to which evaluations are commonly directed, but also screening out issues or questions concerning which no action would result even were an answer to be forthcoming. It is a step away from the research orientation of many evaluation organizations.

The last stage of analysis is to define the information that can be collected about the program represented by the evaluable program model. As opposed to the normal situation in which an evaluator finds himself, he would have relatively firm agreement on the success criteria and underlying logic of the program to be evaluated. He can proceed to define an information package that he can commit himself to produce and deliver to the manager.

It is possible that after analysis of the rhetorical program model, both the evaluable program design and the information that can be collected will be extremely simple--in some cases, trivial. In itself, this fact may be important feedback to the manager.

5. *PRESENTATION TO THE MANAGER*

The manager of the program will have contributed his time to an assessment of his program, and the information derived must be given to him in a form that is useful for determination of next steps. The information he needs is:

- the rhetorical model--an accurate descriptive model of his program reflecting both interviews and documentation;
- the evaluable model--the evaluator's assessment of the program that is being managed and can be evaluated;

- explanation of the analytical process that led to the evaluable model; and

- potential information that could be collected in relation to performance as defined in the evaluable model.

The presentation should be aimed at the following:

- *Obtaining agreement or further clarification of the program design.* There may well be differences of opinion or judgment concerning the measurability of specific objectives or the underlying program logic. The presentation affords the program manager the opportunity to clarify any objectives, or questions of design logic. The exchange of views between the evaluator and the manager is important, since he will be a major potential user of any information produced.

- *Determining the manager's need for the information that can be collected.* During the presentation, the evaluator will define the type of information he can produce. It is a management judgment whether or not that information is needed. The evaluator can and should suggest ways in which the information might be of use, but only in rare instances will the evaluator actually use the information. The manager is positioned to use it and must make the final decision. Keep in mind, however, that there will often be more than one manager concerned with use. The fact that a branch or division manager sees no utility does not preclude an agency manager from assuming the position of major user.

- *Determining to what extent the manager perceives the need to modify his program design.* Whether the findings of the evaluability assessment indicate the need to redesign the program will depend upon the manager's objectives. If he intends to accomplish objectives that are implausible, given his current design, he will change the design or give up the objectives, depending on the constraints on his action authority.

D. IMPLICATIONS—WHAT DO WE DO NEXT?

The evaluability assessment, as indicated earlier, should assist both the evaluator and the manager.

1. EVALUATION PLANNING

Certainly at least one part of an evaluation manager's job is to provide information about programs to the managers of those programs. In theory, at least, this feedback process is supposed to result in better decisions, resulting in turn in more effective programs. The findings of the evaluability assessment will focus the attention of the evaluator on information that can be collected about the activities and objectives for which agreement already exists concerning success measures. The evaluation planning base is a well-defined program.

The evaluator must still concern himself with the utility of the information. The last task prior to evaluation design would then be to define--with the program manager--the intended utility of the information that can be gathered by evaluation studies of the program. Although, again in theory, the place to begin such a definition of utility is in the decision process, we have found only rare situations in which a program manager could explicate his decision process in a way that facilitated evaluation. The process of defining intended use with the program manager can help the manager clarify the criteria that he himself might use to initiate actions. Even imprecise definitions of use will let the evaluator know how accurate the information needs to be, thereby at least partially establishing the scope of the study.

2. *PROGRAM PLANNING*

Program managers often correctly perceive the limitations on their authority to modify programs that have been authorized by Congress. Yes, it is possible to prepare modified legislation, but the path to approval is long and complex and involves many actions beyond the reach of the manager's influence. The manager does have control over his internal resources: staff, R & D funds, and evaluation funds. If we accept the concept of a program design as including both the objects of legislation (e.g., service centers, clinics, etc.) and some set of federal activities, then the manager's most likely influence over the program will be through his internal resources. He has real, even if finite, options. His resources might be applied to:

- research,
- technical assistance,
- information systems, and
- regulations and guidelines.

The evaluability assessment should provide insights into the relationship between his internal activities and the program objectives he would like to achieve. Program redesign may be indicated if the evaluability assessment reveals that there are no plausible links between his research program and his objectives, if technical assistance cannot be shown to be effective in terms of his objectives, or if his staff activities generally appear to be ends in themselves. The real test of whether or not program redesign is warranted is not the finding of the assessment but, rather, the manager's reaction. Should he believe that his program activities are worthwhile as presently constituted, then no redesign is warranted (from his perspective).

One of the more important findings of such assessments may be the identification of serious differences among managers (branch, division, agency, for example) as to the objectives of the program. The assessment cannot resolve those differences, but can serve as a useful communications device to point out to all concerned wherein the differences lie. In this instance, information would be used to stimulate action by the cognizant managers to resolve important areas of difference.

APPENDIX B

Rapid Feedback Evaluation

RAPID FEEDBACK EVALUATION

A. WHAT IS RAPID FEEDBACK EVALUATION?

Program evaluation compares the program as defined by management with reality: the activities and results actually occurring. A rapid feedback evaluation is a program evaluation which uses readily available or readily obtainable information. The products of a rapid feedback evaluation are:

- a formal definition of the program developed through an assessment of evaluability;
- a bounding of the program's cost, outputs, and effects, using available information;
- identification of further evaluation studies that might be useful to management; and
- estimation of the cost and feasibility of carrying out these evaluations.

A rapid feedback evaluation produces a preliminary assessment of the program *and* information to determine if present knowledge (when assembled) is sufficient for management's needs. It provides management with a synthesis of what is known and a set of options for future information purchases if the current knowledge base is judged inadequate. Compared to a full evaluation effort, it is completed relatively quickly (three to six months) and is relatively inexpensive (five to ten manmonths of effort).

B. WHY CONDUCT RAPID FEEDBACK EVALUATIONS?

There are two reasons for conducting rapid feedback evaluations: (1) to enable the evaluation planner to develop useful evaluation information systematically, and (2) to enable program management to stop information collection at a point where its information needs have been met, given the constraints of feasibility, time, and money.

1. *EVALUATION PLANNING*

Experience has shown that program evaluation is a time-consuming and expensive endeavor. It is not unusual for evaluation studies to take well over a year or more with total costs on the order of $1 million. At the same time, the utility and quality of the evaluation product has frequently been questioned both by government officials and by the social science research community.

The evaluation planner within a government agency faces a number of serious constraints in developing high-quality, useful information.

- *Timing:* The nature of the government decision process usually calls for information on a short-time basis--three to six months. Political issues and high-level government personnel change frequently, often leaving no audience or priority need for a long-term evaluation study when it is completed.

- *Feasibility:* Evaluations in the field often require significant methodological development work to carry out the study. In many cases, it is found that, with the current state-of-the-art, evaluation is not feasible. The result is an inconclusive study.

- *Program ambiguity:* A major cause of the low use of evaluation is that most social programs are not sufficiently well-defined to produce agreement among management as to success criteria. This lack of agreement is manifested in the form of criticism after the fact with the method and findings of evaluation studies.

- *User ambiguity:* Another factor contributing to low use is ambiguity on the part of management as to how they would use, or why they need, certain information. Evaluations are funded, completed, and given limited dissemination with no consideration to how it will be used. This frequently results in information which management does not have the authority, resources, or expertise to act upon.

An evaluation effort may ultimately fail for any one of the above reasons--some of which are beyond the direct control of the evaluation planner.

Rapid feedback evaluation enables the evaluator to deal with these constraints by producing information quickly, assessing program and user ambiguity, and estimating the cost, feasibility, and utility of future information purchases. It is most useful when management is in a hurry for evaluative information on a program and when there is the possibility that an expensive evaluation study may be undertaken in the future.

2. *MANAGEMENT*

Agency management makes decisions about their programs with or without information. While many decisions can be anticipated (e.g., what budget level will be recommended), the criteria on which decisions will be made frequently cannot. Managers find themselves in an uncertain world regarding what information they require, what information is feasible to produce, and, strangely enough, what is already known about the program (e.g., the extent and quality of the existing information base).

Rapid feedback evaluation provides the manager, within a short time frame, a synthesis of what is currently known about the program and an assessment of what can be known (in the form of feasible evaluation designs). It can reduce his uncertainty about the program, its operations, and its performance and provide a basis for both program design and information purchase decisions.

C. HOW IS A RAPID FEEDBACK EVALUATION CARRIED OUT?

Rapid feedback evaluation is a sequential series of activities which involve both the evaluator and management. The steps are as follows:

- *Assessment of program evaluability:* Determining whether the program, as defined by management, is sufficiently unambiguous to permit evaluations to be carried out and used.

- *Collection of information:* Gathering readily available information on program costs, operations and results from past studies, data systems, knowledgeable people, and project sites.

- *Bounding program variables:* Synthesis of available information to estimate the possible magnitude of program costs, operating levels, and effects.

- *Analysis of evaluation feasibility and utility:* Determining to what extent future evaluations would be methodologically feasible and useful to management.

- *Presentation to management:* Communication of the rapid feedback evaluation results to program management and determination of next steps to be taken.

1. ASSESSMENT OF PROGRAM EVALUABILITY

Evaluability assessment produces a framework of program definitions, assumptions and intentions which is used in all of the four subsequent steps. Its product is a formal definition of the program (called "the evaluable program model") and the identification of possible evaluation studies that might be useful to management.

The evaluability assessment is carried out through a number of interactions between the evaluator and management. The evaluator works with management to produce a rhetorical program model--a description of the program which captures all program activities and objectives as defined by management. The evaluator then applies two criteria to the rhetorical model to produce an evaluable model: (a) *those in charge of the program have agreed to measurable objectives;* and (b) *those in charge of the program have established testable assumptions linking application of resources to program activities, and linking program activities to program objectives.*

All objectives and assumptions which cannot meet these criteria of "measurability" and "testability" are removed from the rhetorical model. The resulting "evaluable" program model reflects management's intention *and* those program objectives and assumptions which may be tested through evaluation. The evaluator, with the evaluable model, can now define the information that can be collected.

The final step in the evaluability assessment is the evaluator's presentation of the results to management in order to (1) obtain their agreement on the assessment or further clarification on the program, and (2) determine their need for and use of the evaluation information that can be collected. Here the evaluator introduces a third criterion into the evaluability assessment: Do those in charge of the program have the motivation, ability, and authority to use evaluation information? At this point, management may identify evaluation information which it has no use for, thereby reducing the set of possible evaluations to be considered in future design work.

2. *COLLECTION OF INFORMATION*

Once the evaluable program model is agreed upon, it is used to organize and guide information collection efforts. Information is sought on all variables identified in the evaluable model.

Logical sources of information are past evaluations, program reporting systems, project sites, program staff, and other knowledgeable people. Rapid feedback evaluation attempts to use both quantitative and qualitative information. For example, the opinions and views of people knowledgeable about the program are often a valuable source of information. This type of information can be systematically collected and incorporated into the analysis.

Secondary data sources, such as completed studies, will be heavily relied upon. However, depending on the nature of the program, the information collection effort may require site visits or special surveys. For example, actual program activity, such as projects in the field, might be visited and modeled to determine the degree to which the program is implemented as designed.

Telephone surveys might be used to collect information from project sites or people expert in the program area. Any such collection effort would have to be designed and completed quickly (one month), thereby limiting the scope of what can be undertaken. The intention of rapid feedback evaluation is to rely on readily available *and* readily obtainable information rather than to expand the current knowledge base.

3. *BOUNDING THE PROGRAM VARIABLES*

The next step in the analysis is to use the information collected to estimate the magnitude of the variables (cost, output, effects) defined in the evaluable model. This amounts to mapping out what is known about the program and how well it is known.

The evaluator is not expected to say definitively what the program results are; rather, he is trying to bound the range within which effects are likely to fall. A number of possible approaches can be used in synthesizing available information. Past measurement results may be sufficient to estimate ranges with known degrees of confidence. In the absence of any empirical evidence, the evaluator might consider what the program results would be, given the worst possible case and the best possible case. The evaluator might also estimate ranges based on the opinion of knowledgeable observers. In any case, the source and quality of the information on which the estimates are based would be noted.

The product of this step is a preliminary assessment of the program. It is the best estimate of costs and performance, given the current state of knowledge.

4. *ANALYSIS OF EVALUATION FEASIBILITY AND UTILITY*

In Steps 1 through 3, the evaluator has developed (a) a model of the program acceptable to management, (b) a set of possible evaluation studies which management views as useful, and (c) estimates of the ranges of program variables and parameters. With this information, the evaluator can estimate the likely cost and methodological feasibility of these evaluations while exploring further the utility of such information to management.

The issues and approaches involved in estimating cost and feasibility will depend on the type of studies involved. For example, in evaluating the impact of manpower training on national unemployment rates, the issue might be: How large must a national sample survey be to detect with confidence the differences in unemployment rates expected to be attributable to the program? On the other hand, for a monitoring system the issue might be the cost and practicality of establishing a standard project-based data system. In any event, there will be a range of technical issues with cost-feasibility implications which the evaluator can address to further screen and develop evaluation proposals. The result of this step is an evaluation study design for those studies which are cost-feasible.

The evaluator can now test further the utility of the proposed evaluations to management. For example, he might develop samples of likely study results, present them to management, and ask them to describe how they would act upon the information. On the basis of such iterations, the evaluator can rank evaluation proposals and designs on their potential utility.

5. *PRESENTATION TO MANAGEMENT*

The information developed in the rapid feedback evaluation must be presented to management in a form that is useful for deciding upon next steps. The information that should be presented includes:

- *the rhetorical model*--an accurate descriptive model of the program as defined by management;
- *the evaluable model*--the evaluator's description of the program that is being managed and can be evaluated;
- *preliminary program evaluation*--an assessment of the program based on available information; and
- *evaluation study designs*--a description of the cost, feasibility, and utility of further program evaluations.

The presentation should be aimed at the following:

- *Program decisions by management*. The assessment of evaluability and the preliminary program evaluation may lead management to alter the program--its design or its budget.
- *Information purchase decisions by management*. Given the review of existing knowledge and the assessment of what new knowledge can reasonably be produced, management is in a position to decide whether or not it requires more program evaluation information.

D. IMPLICATIONS--WHAT DO WE DO NEXT?

Rapid feedback evaluation should assist both the evaluator and management in making program decisions and information purchase decisions.

1. *PROGRAM PLANNING*

Managers are often limited in their authority to modify programs that have been authorized by Congress. Managers do have a traditional role in recommending and defending program budget levels and they do have control over their internal resources--staff, research and development funds, evaluations funds, and so on. It is in these two areas that program and agency managers exert their greatest influence.

The rapid feedback evaluation provides management with an information base that describes the relationship between internal resources, program activities, program objectives, and program budget levels. This type of analysis can point out many problems which can be acted upon by management. For example:

- serious differences between managers (branch, division agency, etc.) as to the objectives of the program;
- no plausible links between staff activities and program objectives;
- no plausible link between evaluation and research efforts and program objectives;
- marked differences between field projects and the evaluable program model (the program as defined by management);
- program objectives which are unattainable; and
- program activities which have not been implemented.

Management response to such problems might involve internal redesign of the program by the staff or may result in new legislative and budgetary proposals to Congress.

2. *EVALUATION PLANNING*

The evaluation planner has always been faced with a dilemma--a high demand for evaluation information, but very little guidance on which of the many possible evaluation studies to undertake. Expectations for evaluation have been unreasonably high in the past, driving evaluators to undertake many unfeasible high-risk studies.

Rapid feedback evaluation provides the evaluator with a framework--a set of decision criteria--for guiding evaluation planning. It requires that he interact with management to lay out the set of potentially useful studies and to synthesize available knowledge as a basis for estimating feasibility.

At the end of a rapid feedback evaluation, the evaluation planner is in a sound position to determine how much of his resources—such as staff time and budget—he is willing to put into further evaluative work on the program. Generally, several courses of action are open:

- cease further evaluation work on the program;
- work with management to redesign the program so that the resulting design is evaluable; and
- undertake further evaluations of the program as it currently exists.

The major consideration in selecting a course of action will be the response of management to the rapid feedback evaluation.

APPENDIX C

*Definition of Federal Evaluation
Adopted by a DHEW Task Force on Health Evaluation**

*Policies and Procedures for Evaluation of Health Programs: I. Seeman, March 11, 1975 (DHEW/ASPE draft health evaluation policy).

The following activities are to be considered as federal evaluation.

1. Assessment of national health programs.

2. Assessment of demonstration programs which have major implication for programs with national scope.

3. Analysis of assessment of program or management processes, procedures, intervention techniques or activities, excepting only those specific to a single local project.

4. Analysis or assessment of existing policies to determine their impact upon programmatic activities, but excluding assessment of prospective policies.

5. The design and/or development of general evaluation methodologies, as well as such methodology as may be developed for assessment of specific programs. Further, support for development of methodologies, which may be implemented by other than the federal government to assess an individual project (i.e., "project specific), is appropriate, and may include preparation of project evaluation manuals or handbooks for grantees. The execution of these methodologies to evaluate individual local projects, however, is not included.

6. Assessment and analysis of program designs; activities devoted to securing more evaluable program designs.

7. The initial design and development of management information systems for programs of national scope.

8. Securing of technical assistance to aid in or related to evaluation of eligible programs, excluding, however, assistance to a single local project.

9. Development and pilot testing of instruments and procedures whose purpose is on-site project review and monitoring. The monitoring process itself, however, is not included.

10. Short-term training of federal employees whose professional concern is primarily evaluation of programs.

The following types of activities are *not* considered as federal evaluation:

1. The assessment of individual local projects.

2. The assessment of individual experiments and demonstrations.

3. The continuing operation of management information systems.

4. The continuing collection of baseline data.

5. On-site review and monitoring of local projects.

6. Basic research, health services research and policy research.